At Speed

W. SCOTT OLSEN

At Speed

Traveling the Long Road
between Two Points

University of Nebraska Press ∾ Lincoln & London

Source acknowledgments for previously
published material appear on p. ix.

Library of Congress Cataloging-in-Publication Data
Olsen, W. Scott, 1958–
At speed: traveling the long road between two points /
W. Scott Olsen.
p. cm.
ISBN-13: 978-0-8032-3581-6 (cloth: alk. paper)
ISBN-10: 0-8032-3581-X (cloth: alk. paper)
1. United States—Description and travel.
2. United States—History, Local.
3. Olsen, W. Scott, 1958–   —Travel—United States.
4. Travel—Psychological aspects.   5. Motion—
Psychological aspects.   I. Title.
E169.Z83O44   2006
917.304′931—dc22
2006001131

For Maureen, Kate, and Andrew

Exploration is the physical expression of the Intellectual Passion. And I tell you, if you have the desire for knowledge and the power to give it physical expression, go out and explore. If you are a brave man you will do nothing: if you are fearful you may do much, for none but cowards have need to prove their bravery. Some will tell you that you are mad, and nearly all will say, "What is the use?" For we are a nation of shopkeepers, and no shopkeeper will look at research which does not promise him a financial return within a year. And so you sledge nearly alone, but those with whom you sledge will not be shopkeepers: that is worth a good deal. If you march your Winter Journeys you will have your reward, so long as all you want is a penguin's egg.

APSLEY CHERRY-GARRARD, *The Worst Journey in the World*

For, d'ye see, rainbows do not visit the clear air; they only irradiate vapor. And so, through all the thick mists of the dim doubts in my mind, divine intuitions now and then shoot, enkindling my fog with a heavenly ray. And for this I thank God; for all have doubts; many deny; but doubts or denials, few along with them, have intuitions. Doubts of all things earthly, and intuitions of some things heavenly; this combination makes neither believer nor infidel, but makes a man who regards them both with equal eye.

HERMAN MELVILLE, *Moby-Dick*

Even at a standstill you can feel it inside you. The road as verge, as threshold, making "destination" a mere pretext for the real business of going to meet it.

REG SANER, "The Road's Motion"

CONTENTS

ACKNOWLEDGMENTS

Many people helped bring this book to life, and to each of them I am deeply grateful. The fine people at Concordia College in Moorhead, Minnesota, where I work, as well as the Jerome Foundation and the Lake Region Arts Council, were generous with their help to fund these trips, and without their support none of these chapters would have been possible. Alexis Hurley, my agent, and Robert Taylor, my editor at Nebraska, both believed in this project, and their insights were substantial. "The Road in Winter" originally appeared in *Third Coast*, no. 19, Fall 2004, and to the editors there I offer special thanks. In the course of my after-trip writing, people far too many to mention—from university faculty to historical society staffers to gas station clerks—suffered my phone calls as I tried to track down some small bits of information or history, and likewise, a thousand Web sites with unseen contributors and managers helped fill in the holes in my limited notes. Finally, to every person I met on these trips who told me a story or helped me see where I was, my profound thanks.

At Speed

The Climb

Your inquiry to the U.S. Geological Survey's Earth Science Information Center was referred to the Geographic Names Office for reply. No, the U.S. Geological Survey does not, nor does any Federal agency, have an official definition for mountain, hill, or any other generic term as used with geographic names. In fact, there are no official Federal definitions for these terms as they apply to geographic features. In the naming process these terms are purely perceptive or application driven. Various agencies may have internal definitions that are application driven, but none are used universally or are official. The reason is perception and function. People perceive features differently, and the need or functional classification is often the driving force. For example, is the feature called a river based on length, volume of water, or some other criterion? A water resources office may have one need while local perception may be totally different. Usually, streams are hierarchical in concept, but very close to us here in Reston, Virginia, Little River flows into Goose Creek, which is very unsettling to many. Similarly, the difference between a mountain and a hill is well known to everyone except that it differs from place to place and even group-to-group. The 63 categories available in our type of feature list were developed by us specifically to facilitate search and retrieval of entries having similar characteristics, and we attempted to select very general terms that are not controversial, hence summit for all uplifted features since, for example, mountain or hill creates confusion and unending argument. In fact there are 190 different generic terms that fit the definition of summit, some are quite rare and unusual. You may be interested to know that the

British Ordnance Survey once defined a mountain as having 1,000 feet of elevation, and less was a hill. This was the definition at the time on which the movie *The Englishman Who Went Up a Hill and Down a Mountain* was based. You might recall that the summit in question was the first elevated feature which one encounters upon entering Wales from England, and it was very important to the local folk that it be classified a mountain. The British have, we have been informed, abandoned the definition. We are not exactly sure when the British abandoned their definition (possibly the 1920s). The U.S. Board on Geographic Names once stated that the difference between a hill and a mountain was 1,000 feet of local relief, but even this was abandoned in the early 1970s.

ROGER L. PAYNE, Executive Secretary,
U.S. Board on Geographic Names

Six o'clock in the morning and I am standing on dry land, 282 feet below sea level. A short distance behind me, a small spring brings water to the surface—water far too salty to drink. The temperature is 112 degrees above zero.

This is Death Valley, California. A spot called Badwater. The lowest spot in the whole of North America. White salt dust covers my boots. There is no breeze this morning, and no sound other than the crunch of my footfalls. Although I can see my Jeep at the pullout where I parked, now some distance to the east, no other traffic moves along Route 178, the small road that hugs the edge where the flats meet the sharp rise of earth. Beyond the roadway, the Black Mountains still hide the rising sun.

The temperature this morning is more than I am used to, but the sun has not yet filled the valley floor and the air is pleasant, almost sweet with the smells of plants and flowers in the hills. There is the smell of salt, too. Everywhere I look, my eye is filled with the residue of hard baking.

I watch the sunlight move down the mountains on the western edge of the valley, the browns and blacks and grays of the Panamint Range, places with names like Starvation Canyon and Telescope Peak, and I smile when a small dramatic voice in my head says I should be running from this sunlight and the possibly lethal heat it will bring. But I do not run. Even though I hope to end this day a long way from here, for now I have water in my pack and air-conditioning in the Jeep. And I am slow to move away from the one truth this morning already holds. Badwater, at sunrise, is a beautiful place.

Of course, I have no good reason for being here. No good reason other than curiosity, and a desire to know what sense might be made from connections. I read maps the way other people read novels—every road line its own narrative, every town name a character, every border a twist in the plot. And some time ago, I'm not really sure when, I found myself holding a small leather-bound directory of national parks, each with its own colored map. I was looking at the map for Death Valley National Park, only because I knew the lowest spot on the continent was there, and I was tracing the road line when a question came up. There is a road, I saw, at Badwater. That makes it the lowest roadway in North America. So where, then, was the highest? I knew the highest peaks (Denali for North America and Mount Whitney—only eighty miles from Death Valley—for the lower forty-eight states), but where was the highest roadway? How high could I drive?

It wasn't an easy question. Though after a flurry of emails and phone calls, I had a partial answer. Mount Evans, outside Denver, boasts the highest *paved* road in North America. 14,264 feet above sea level. What about Forest Service roads, I asked? What about dirt roads, unpaved roads, drivable trails? The Forest Service could not tell me, or if they could they did not want to. I asked the U.S. Geological Survey too. But they have little interest in roads. The Department of Transportation told me to call the Forest Service, and so around I went. Finally, paved was good enough for me.

Badwater to Mount Evans, I thought. 14,546 feet of vertical distance. Looking at a road atlas, I began to smile. They are not that far apart— nine hundred miles, give or take a bit. Certainly doable. Perhaps, if I started early enough, I could finish in just one day; I could connect the lowest and the highest. What would I see along the way? What would I think and feel, starting at the bottom and ending at the top? What would I learn about the shape of the land if I could go from one to the other?

I couldn't say when, but I knew I'd be going.

So, I'm here only because Badwater, the lowest spot in the Western

Hemisphere, has one of those odd calls to my imagination—a special place because it's extreme. It is a place I had to see, that I had to touch and taste and muddy my boots with. Mount Evans, at the end of this day, though very different, appeals for the very same reason. And there is the distance between them, the process of nine hundred miles over and three miles up, the story that comes from seeing the earth rise and fall and rise again, the questions that spring like storms in the summer sky, and the memory to hold forever.

This morning, the mountains of the Panamint Range turn pink in the early morning light. A few cotton-ball clouds frame Telescope Peak, itself 11,049 feet above sea level. A half-moon seems to rest lightly in the sky. Behind me, the Black Mountains on the east side of the valley remain dark and hard and large. And there is no sound here this morning—no birdcall, no wind, no rushing water. Slowly, wanting both to remain and to go, I walk back to the Jeep, get in, check the supplies, turn the key, put it in gear, and begin.

 ~

Whether it's told or not, every good story has a chapter called "The Night Before." This one is no exception. Last night, I stayed at a place called Stovepipe Wells, thirty miles or so north of Badwater. The whole place is just a gas station, a general store, a small hotel and restaurant, a swimming pool. Old wagon wheels rest against a split rail fence. Behind the store, the dunes begin, brown and soft in the evening light. The place is named Stovepipe Wells because prospectors coming through would dig for water and plant pieces of stovepipe in the ground to mark the holes.

I asked the desk clerk if there was a thermometer, if he knew what the temperature was. He said there was one out by the pool, but he frowned as he told me. "It's one of the new kinds," he said. "It only goes up to 120 degrees." He shook his head and said, "I don't know what they were thinking."

Stovepipe Wells is run by the Park Service. Parts are ordered from somewhere else. I walked outside and looked at the thermometer by the pool. The temperature read 115 degrees, and although the sky was still light the sun had set behind the mountains. "There are many days," he said, "when 120 doesn't even come close."

I put my one bag in the spartan room, walked outside and realized I'd arrived at the wrong time of day. It was too late to head off for a hike in the dunes, too early to turn in. No one was swimming in the pool and there were few other guests in the hotel. I walked around a bit, exploring the outsides of buildings, looking longingly toward the dunes and the mountains and the darkening sky, and eventually I found myself at the general store where the clerk and I only smiled at each other. I'd promised myself I wouldn't ask him about the temperature. Nonetheless, a sign on an outside wall said, "The winter climate is delightful. The valley bakes under a savage summer sun." It said, "Death Valley consistently has the highest temperatures on earth. On July 10, 1913, the weather bureau thermometer at Furnace Creek stood at 134 degrees Fahrenheit, 57 degrees Celsius—a world record for many years. Air temperatures above 120 degrees Fahrenheit/49 Celsius are common in July and August. Ground temperatures can rise above 200 degrees Fahrenheit/93 degrees Celsius. Rocks can become too hot to touch." Then it went on to say, "The summer can take the lives of unfortunate or foolhardy travelers."

I do know a little about compression heating—air that's trapped by the valley walls is heated by the sun and tries to rise, but then it tends to fall back on itself and press down, compressing the lowest layer to the highest temperature—but that was little help as I tried to imagine what a day here would feel like on my neck and arms, and what it would taste like in my lungs. Suddenly thirsty, and with little else to do, I wandered into the restaurant as soon as it opened.

I never met the man, but the cook's name was Lucky. The waitress seated me at a table near a wall, with a good view of both the television and the large picture window, poured me a glass of water and began to tell me what Lucky suggested. "The prime rib, honey, is what I'd order," she said. "Lucky made a big one today, and there aren't enough people to eat it. I've seen what he's serving, and you should trust me on this one."

I went for this special, with a glass of wine, and settled into thoughts about the upcoming day, the long drive, the way light can shift hues as the sun moves from one end of the sky to the other. And I smiled when I noticed that the restaurant, western style, was brown. A long brown bar, with brown bar stools. Brown carpet. Brown tables. Brown chairs.

Brown doors. Outside the window, a view of brown buildings, brown dunes, brown mountains, a darkening blue sky. My white wine, very cold, arrived with the brown meat, a brown potato. And the slice of prime rib was very large.

Despite the fact that what I thought was a small plastic tub of "butter" turned out to be strong horseradish sauce—something I did not discover until I'd mixed it with my baked potato and put a large bite into my mouth—the meal was wonderful. Then I walked outside, in the pleasant mood of a good meal, only to discover emergency vehicles and park ranger trucks racing past Stovepipe Wells.

"Washout," someone said. "Some people are stuck."

I don't know how the news traveled, but the man at the general store seemed to know what was going on. Earlier in the day, a good bit before I arrived, a storm moved through the north end of the valley. Rain fell hard and fast for a very short time, and the cant of the rocks pushed it into valleys, where it gathered and then began to push the rocks themselves. The road north of Stovepipe Wells has rises and then hollows, small dips and crests, and when the flash flood hit the flat of the valley it filled the depressions with mud and boulders and debris. Coming around a corner, drivers found the flat of asphalt turned into the texture of the moon.

"That muck has to be at least fifteen feet deep in places," the man at the store said.

The road to the north was closed. A small band of cars was stuck between two washouts. Ranger trucks sped by Stovepipe Wells every twenty minutes or so, ferrying people back and forth

"There is no travel to the north now. Although to the south should be just fine," the desk clerk said.

A German couple, gray-haired and trim, pulled up in the car they rented in Colorado. They were already guests in the hotel. They had driven up to look at the washout as soon as they heard the news. "The first one isn't bad," the man said. "We didn't drive through it. There are more in the distance."

The woman pointed at a dirty white Mustang convertible parked in the gas station, the owner on his back with his head under the car. "We could see his tracks," the woman said, as if she were sharing a secret.

"He drove through it," the man continued. "First one. Didn't even

6

know it was there. Sixty miles per hour and straight into the mess."

"Like surfing," the woman said, "with the grace of God."

I waited for a semi and flatbed trailer to pass, a large bulldozer on the trailer en route to the cleanup, then walked over to the gas station. The man appeared from under the Mustang and I could hear him talking with the store clerk. "It may be drivable," he said. "But everything under there is trashed."

A park ranger truck and a hotel van arrived, and both let passengers off at the hotel.

I saw one of the hotel employees walking toward the van. I said, "Do you know how many people were stuck?" He said, "No, I don't. But, they figure than can fit all the remaining ones in one van." The guy in the van took off north.

At the hotel, even though the sun had set, the temperature was still over 100 degrees. The tourists, as they were ferried back, filled the small hotel registration area. Some of them were sunburned bikers: Harley t-shirts, leather jackets, dark glasses. Many of them were overweight men suddenly out of their air-conditioning. One wore a Mickey Mouse shirt. Another pair was German. One couple was Italian. Somewhere in the background I heard someone speaking French, too. All of them smiled, all of them told stories of their adventure, glad to be rescued at day's end.

Two men I met in the small courtyard of the hotel were talking as I walked by. I said, "Were you stuck?"

They both smiled and said, "Yes, we were!"

"A bit of an adventure then?"

"Yes, it was!" and they told me the whole story one more time—the adrenaline a long way from leaving their bodies.

The restaurant where I ate dinner by myself was now packed with the grateful and the hungry—the bar doing extraordinary business. The men and women walked around almost dazed, telling and retelling the story to themselves: where they were, what they saw. None of the stories were very different, of course. Each of them simply reconfirmed that something extraordinary had happened. Everyone ordered the special, and the slices, I saw, grew increasingly thin. Outside, children filled the pool with their bodies and their glee.

Talking with the front desk clerk I learned there were nearly thirty people in the hotel who hadn't planned to be here. Their cars remained stranded between the washouts. One of the stranded men reported he had talked to the operator of the road cleaning equipment and sixteen hours was his estimate to clear the road.

Not one of the new guests had seen a drop of rain, they said. Clouds, yes. And then a road that was not there. No one complained. This was an adventure in Death Valley, and they were rescued fast.

～

South of Badwater, the white salt flats near the mountains take on the appearance of water. The valley floor is a flat plain of tumbled rocks. When the light changes, if I didn't know better, the white salt of the flats would look like snow. The road south out of Badwater hugs the mountain face, heads west into the valley to skirt an alluvial fan, then curves east back to the rock. These are the oldest rocks in Death Valley, 1.8 billion years old, the dolomite and volcanic base of the Black Mountains.

It's a wonderful drive.

Almost up to speed, then I hit the brakes as I find a washout even here in the south end of the valley. I did not see the rain, but this end of the valley is wet. Yesterday's storms moved rock and gravel over the road, and the road is half-covered by water. The depressions at the shoulders are filled with runoff—not yet evaporated by the morning sun racing toward me. Judging from the size of the rocks and the amount of mud carried across the roadway, the flash floods here must be spectacular.

6:35 a.m. Morning Point, the sign says. Elevation: sea level.

6:46 a.m. I've lost the race with the sun. Coming around a bend, the mountains in the distance are a bit lower, a bit farther away, and so sunshine floods the valley. It may be just my imagination, but I feel the temperature instantly rise. I pass a small sign that says, "How vivid is your imagination? Can you visualize the desert scene below you as it would have appeared approximately 20,000 years ago? Imagine if you can this valley filled with a lake 90 miles long, 6 to 11 miles wide and 600 feet deep."

A guidebook tells me this valley may have filled, and dried, more than twenty times as ice-ages came and left, or much earlier as the Sierra Nevadas erupted and rose to create a rainshadow where there once was an inland sea. Most recently, meltwater from the Sierra Nevadas ran into this valley, and others to the north. Lake Manley, the southernmost in a chain of lakes, would have found its small waves ending just here.

Today, though, I pass a sign that tells me I can get radiator water in one mile.

6:50 a.m. The southern road out of Death Valley finally turns east, starts to head up into the mountains toward Shoshone and then Las Vegas. The engine pulls, the road rises. I still have a long way to go.

$\sim$

At Jubilee Pass, 1,293 feet above sea level, the road twists and begins a descent on the far side. Sage grasses and wildflowers fill the open spaces beyond both shoulders.

It's impossible to describe the sight of Death Valley behind me. The tremendous space opening up, going farther down than you imagine the earth should or ever would. As when you're standing at the edge of a canyon or cliff, or even on the roof of a tall building, there seems to be some pull, some urge toward falling in or over. I pull the Jeep to the side of the road and get out to take in the view. I feel as if I'm leaving something unfinished. But the road on the east side of Jubilee Pass descends into a small valley of its own, with its own pull and its own small urgings, so once again the Jeep is in a forward gear. Not far over the southern horizon, I know, the antennae of NASA's Deep Space Network bring into radio view a much larger void.

At 7:03 in the morning, I pass a sign that says, Elevation 3,000 Feet. The roadway cuts through some rock, the exposed layers of sediment folded and bent. A moment later I pass another sign. Salsberry Pass— Elevation 3,315 Feet. I already know that if you type in the names of these passes as a Web search, you get stories and pictures from bicycle races that start in Furnace Creek or Badwater and turn around here, or stories and pictures about hunts for "ephemeral" wildflowers, fields of yellow against the desert brown. But up and running now, I'm more focused on the sign that says "Five percent downgrade next four miles."

Ten minutes later I leave Death Valley National Park. Still heading east in the mountains, dark and silhouetted against the rising sun, fold after fold of mountain rising then falling, I pass a sign that reads "Elevation 2,000 Feet." And then a town appears. Shoshone, California. Population: 100, elevation 1,572 feet. A small town, mostly trailer homes and a gas station where a gallon is fifty cents more expensive than any-where else I've seen, not a soul is outside though a sign at the station says it's open.

I'm over the Black Mountains, I think, and on to something else. No going back now. I press on the gas and smile as my body feels the accel-eration. California 178 east of Shoshone is the Charles Brown Highway.

~

7:34 a.m. Welcome to Nevada! First town: Pahrump. Elevation: 2,695 feet.

Coming into Pahrump is much like coming into any town. The out-skirts are filled with auto body, glass and paint shops. Trailer homes. Small houses built on slabs. Fast food. Gas stations. Billboards for real estate, billboards for hotels and casinos. There is a billboard for Jesus and a billboard for the Madame Butterfly Bath and Massage Salon. A sign says this is part of the "New Old West." A cactus near the road flies red, white, and blue American flags that look like Christmas ornaments, ribbons and streamers.

But this is still the desert. Most of the ground is brown dirt and sand, sun-scorched dust and rock. It's only 90 degrees now, but the day is already painfully bright and hard. Whatever rain I missed yesterday fell here too. Dirt and mud, spread out into the streets like river deltas or silt plains, makes driving a small adventure. The downpour must have been spectacular, I think, and I wish I'd seen it.

Yet this is no place for stopping. A right turn at a traffic light where I wait for a rusted pickup truck with a bumper sticker that reads "Enough Is Enough—Anyone but Bush," and I'm soon up to speed.

East out of Pahrump the road is four-lane, divided highway—a fall into another broad valley. This one filled with cactus, Joshua trees, yucca plants. Then up again into the mountains. This is basin and range country. Beautiful and stark. I pass an exit for the Spring Mountains National Recreation Area. "316,000 acres of remarkable beauty and sur-prising diversity," a Web site tells me. Another says, "Hikers to the area are introduced to the bristlecone pine (*Pinus longaeva*), a plant consid-ered to be the oldest known living thing in the world. Several specimens have been found which approach 5000 years in age. A bristlecone pine six feet tall may contain as many as 900 growth rings."

And I will admit, happily, there is a part of me that thinks I should be stopping, thinks I should get out of this car and walk, that I should find a bristlecone pine and sit down in front of it, that I should be patient and more focused and deep. It is possible, I know, to live a life that's a mile wide and only an inch deep. But I also know that comparison is the richest source of insight, and stories are the bedrock of culture. Curiosity, fresh as well as satisfied, is its own deep well.

8:17 a.m. Mountain Spring Summit marks the end of the Pahrump Valley, elevation 5,490 feet above sea level, and a Smokey the Bear sign tells me the fire danger is extreme today. Nearly every western state has some type of large scale fire. According to a map I have, printed from the National Interagency Fire Center, there are fifty-two large incident fires in the country today, fires with names like 18 Fire, Fawn Peak Complex, McGinnis Flats, Hot Creek, Wedge Canyon, Black Frog Complex, Deep Lake, Weathead, Maverick, Balcony House Complex and Ditch Creek. By definition, "large incident" fires are more than one hundred acres. In reality, they are much much more. Comparing the fire map and the road atlas, I count nine fires close to my road today. How close, I do not know. Men and women in the hills carrying combination tools called Pulaskis, helicopters with buckets, airplanes with bellies full of retardant; I can't see any of them from here. But the news of them comes through my radio and my reading, and I can imagine them here, in this place, too.

I am passing through the Red Rock Canyon Conservation area. The northern limit of the Joshua tree. Home of the Keystone thrust fault and Aztec sandstone that geologists say were once costal sand dunes nearly three hundred feet tall. Howard Hughes used to own it all, but sold it to the Nevada park system in 1967. Sheets of paper in a notebook on the passenger seat—sheets that hold print-offs of Web sites—tell me these details. Bring water and a good pair of hiking boots, they say. You'll want to get out of your car. And I do want to get out. I want to get out at nearly every bend in the road. But there is another bend in the road up ahead, and I have not seen what's there yet. The pull of what I have not seen is stronger than any other desire in the universe.

8:20 a.m. Coming off a small summit, I can see in the distance, over two small rises in the hills, the towers and the glitter of Las Vegas. Striking, yes. Memorable, and inescapable. But not uncomplicated or untroubling. It's like seeing a police car or an ambulance stopped by the side of the road with the lights flashing. You know there is trouble, and trouble you are glad to avoid. But you cannot help but look as you slow to nearly a crawl and eventually pass.

The land between here and there is gorgeous. Toward the city, the mountains give way to more foothills, tops more rounded than jagged. In my rear-view mirrors I can see the hard rock of two mountains with their pinnacles and cliffs. In front of me, sand and desert and dreams. This portion of the highway, I read, is sponsored by Speedy Sprinkler Repair.

～

8:40 in the morning. A broad turn of the pavement and the road numbers change. I am now on Interstate 15 north. In the distance, brown and green and deep blue peaks. A little closer, the white-brown sand of desert. But right in front of me, the next five exits are for the Las Vegas strip. Even from the interstate, I can make out Mandalay Bay, the MGM Grand, Frank Sinatra Drive, billboards for Natalie Cole, and the Eagles, the Striptease Gentlemen's Club, the Blue Man Group. I'm passed by a black limousine, then a bright yellow stretch Hummer limousine. I can see the Luxor with its pyramid, the Monte Carlo, the Bellagio. The Bellagio is advertising Andy Warhol's celebrity portraits in the Bellagio Gallery of Fine Art. Then there's Cirque de Soleil. A sign for the University of Nevada, Las Vegas. Billboards for Siegfried and Roy as well as Lord of the Dance and, of course, Wayne Newton. The Stardust. Circus Circus.

I have this fantasy, of course. It's the same one we all have. I pull up to some casino, walk in, place just one nickel, or quarter, or perhaps silver dollar in some out-of-the-way slot machine, pull the handle, and smile as the lights begin to flash and the horns begin to sound and a million dollars falls into my lap. Just one coin is all it takes. Just one coin and I could kiss good-bye the trouble with my checkbook every month. Just one coin, and life would be easy. And if not just one coin, perhaps the first was only a warm-up. The second coin is sure to hit. And if not the second, perhaps the third. Just getting into the groove of the machine now, letting it know who I am. Just getting the proper psychic alignments going. Maybe it's the tenth coin, or the hundredth. But I know this baby's going to pay for me. All I need to do is sit here and feed it money. Pretty soon it will pay me back. I can feel it in my bones.

I step on the accelerator. There is a lot not to like about Las Vegas. Even without the silliness of gambling, the problems when play is writ in oversized letters, there is the simple consumption of water, of electricity, of food and everything else. There should not be a city here at all, I think, and I am glad to leave it behind.

Even so, on the north side of Las Vegas, by the motor speedway, when the exit for Nellis Air Force Base appears, I pull off the highway and into a Petro gas station. I fill the Jeep, then walk inside the convenience store to buy a bottle of water. Just for grins, I put one dollar in a video poker machine. I win ten dollars.

Even at a Petro station, at the end of the line of machines there is a counter and an attendant, an old woman, late sixties I'd guess, lively, gray-haired and happily loud. She walks up and down the line of players, commenting on everyone's next best play, patting a few on the back as she relieves herself of her insights. "Wow," she cries, loudly, when I cash out after my first play. She waves her arms over her head in a little mock celebration. "Nobody's given me a tip yet today! Can't even buy a cup of coffee! Nobody, and I mean nobody, has given me a tip today!" I put in another dollar bill and tell her that whatever I win on this one will be her tip. I settle on the chair and she leans in close over my left shoulder. I'm dealt nothing. Keeping one ace I discard four. I'm dealt nothing again.

"Not even a cup of coffee!" she laughs, now wandering down to some other player. Just one dollar, I think, and I'm walking out with nine.

Back on the highway, back in the desert, mountains in the distance and a little bit of green at the roadside, I watch the sweep and swoop of power lines as they crisscross the landscape. A train parallels the highway, what seems like miles and miles of containers soon to be attached to semis. Soon a sign tells me I'm entering the Moapa Indian Reservation. And shortly thereafter, I pass the exit for Lake Mead and the Valley of Fire.

~

Midmorning in the desert north of Las Vegas. The road begins to rise again, crests, but does not fall into some other valley. Just a higher plateau. The hills to the east are blurry now in a heat haze; the temperature slightly more than one hundred degrees. And there is no wind whatsoever. Smoke rising from a small power plant rises straight up until it disappears.

The Jeep hums along easily. I've got the windows down, the air-conditioning off, and the radio just a background underneath the ear-rush of wind noise. I've never been here before—this particular stretch of highway, this particular opening in the land—but I've been here many times. This is one of those moments when you can almost see the size of the planet, when you can almost taste the seasoning of time. The horizon is no longer a border as much as it is an implication. More of this, it promises, until there is something else. And then more of that, until it changes too. You can almost see the curve, almost understand the whole of the shape. The smell of the air brings its own kind of news, what's going on here and near here, and the symphony I can barely hear, written several hundred years before this morning, connects me with the whole of humanity. Overstated? Hyperbole? Perhaps. But at speed the road asks for larger connections than any one town and any one person. So much land going by so fast and the angles of perception get skewed. Going eighty miles per hour while sitting three feet off the ground is very much like flying, I think, or perhaps even space travel. Scale becomes important.

But reverie is always interrupted. So in the midst of these desert dreams is an oasis, the town of Mesquite, green and lush. Irrigated fields, trees, bushes. A bright vivid green against the red rock of the desert. On the east side of Mesquite the desert presses hard against the watered lots. But in town there is a very green golf course, sand traps, water hazards—the Oasis Golf Club. From the highway, I can see that the golf course has a small waterfall. At the exit there's a Starbuck's coffee and the Casablanca Resort/Casino and Spa, with a sign that says they paid out $71 million in 2002 slot payouts. Fountains and waterfalls grace the front of the hotel. Rooms are from $19.50. The prime rib buffet is $7.77. On the west side of town, though, barren rock, boulders, the red haze of the desert.

11:15 in the morning, and I'm in Arizona now. On the north side of Mesquite, on the Arizona side, sprinklers by the dozens pump water onto the golf course. Where the golf course ends, though, the land turns back to the hard red desert. Then the signs begin. "Curves." "Mountain Gorges Next 11 Miles." "Entering Virgin River Gorge." "Strong Cross Wind Possible Next Four Miles."

The speed limit goes down to fifty-five miles an hour. The highway enters the gorge. Suddenly a left turn and then suddenly a right—S turns, the kind that are fun in a sports car. The gorge is immense, so tall on either side I can't see the top even by straining forward to look up or leaning my head to the left to see out the driver's side window. Kaibab and Toroweap limestones, Quantoweap sandstone, Pakoon dolomite. Just names to me, really. But sedimentary rock I understand, the process at least, and these layers angled forty-five degrees to the highway, expose 300 million years of history.

The gravitas of rock is dramatic. Even though a small sign tells me the elevation here is only 2,000 feet, it's impossible not to feel like this is the arc of something important. These hills and these faces and the river below are an intersection, a meeting point. This is the place where the Great Basin meets the Colorado Plateau, where the Mohave Desert meets the Sonoran. This is a place nearly sacred to rock climbers, with routes called Necessary Evil, Route of All Evil, the Fall of Man, and Erotic Jesus, all on a rock called Blasphemy Wall.

I cannot see the Virgin River from the highway; the hills are that steep. Watch for Animals, the sign says, followed by Watch for Rocks. Emergency Parking Only.

Just before the exit for Cedar Pocket, the gorge ends and the land opens up a little bit. The road still cuts through mountains. A tractor-trailer is pulled over on the southbound side, the driver outside the cab holding a camera up, taking a picture of a red pinnacle behind me. Trucks on the upgrade on the northbound side are slowed by the rise and need to use their flashers. A small crest and then the road starts to go downhill. I pass a Roadway semi pulling three trailers. Three trailers on the downhill grade now. An interesting exercise in inertia and momentum and the stopping power of engines and brakes. Myself: I step on the gas.

~

Welcome to Utah. 11:30 in the morning as I pass two families who have stopped to take pictures of themselves underneath the state welcome sign. They smile and point up at the message. And then Van Morrison is on the radio, the opening to "Smoke from a Distant Fire": "You left me here on the way to paradise . . . " Too good to be anything else but true.

The highway continues north through brown desert changing to white desert, a new mountain range in front. The climb still to come. A sign tells me Interstate 15 is the Veterans Memorial Highway. A little oasis comes and goes, this one the town of St. George with green trees, shrubbery, grass, pretty homes. Then an exit for Zion National Park.

From St. George to Cedar City, volcanoes, old cinder cones, rise in the landscape between cliff faces and hills. Pliocene to Quaternary, I'm told. Volcano Mountain, outside the town of Hurricane, is the source for the basalt flows along the Virgin River.

What stories there are! The town of Hurricane, the Hurricane Cliffs, and the Hurricane Fault were named from an offhand comment made by Erastus Snow, a Mormon Church official, who was caught in a storm here in 1863 while doing a survey for irrigation. The cliffs, two hundred miles long, from the Grand Canyon to the border of this highway, make the western edge of the Colorado Plateau. The fault, a high-angle fault that dips west, still rumbles and groans as part of the Intermountain Seismic Belt. Off to the east, a short distance of course, are the Grand Canyon, Lake Mead, Hoover Dam.

It's a gorgeous day in the desert Southwest. I pass a chain-up area as the road moves toward higher elevation and the hills around me are all covered with pine trees, green and pretty against the earth. At Cedar City I see signs for The Shakespeare Center, the City Bricks National Monument, Southern Utah University as well. I'm 5,623 feet above sea level.

Sometimes awareness comes early, and sometimes it comes late. Sometimes it comes long after the fact, and sometimes it sneaks up behind you, stands there like a friend and simply waits for you to turn around. The Jeep is breezing along so easily I have not been thinking about the highway at all. But from the gorge to here, I-15 has been following the base of a long valley. Fields of green, grasses turning to trees turning to what looks like sage. This is the kind of midsummer drive that's easy to settle into, as easy as a song on the radio from a long time ago, a song you'd forgotten but now remember every word of. This is the southern route of the Old Spanish Trail! This is the mule trail from

Missouri to the Pacific coast. There is a book that calls this the most difficult wagon road in American history. And there is all the history and all the stories before the Europeans needed a trade route. From this day's start to its ending, this is the land of the western Shoshones, the southern Paiutes, the Utes and the Hopis and the Arapahos. Before them, the land of the Mongollons, the Hohokams, the Patayans, and the Anasazis. And before them, the terrible lizards. So many eyes have already seen this valley I see for the first time now.

1:04 p.m. The town of Beaver, Utah, and the exit for Great Basin National Park. I pull off here to get some gas for the Jeep and some water for me and find myself itching to get back going fast. Still a long way to go, I think. I can't say I'm worried about the time or the timing yet, but on the entrance ramp I find myself pulling through the gears a bit more quickly than I usually do—and I tend to drive fast.

Still, if the second law of thermodynamics is that all things tend toward chaos, then there must be a law somewhere down the line that says some things tend toward coincidence. Just north of the town of Beaver, I pass through a great big speed trap. A full half dozen highway patrol and sheriff's cars are looking for speeders. One officer has a car stopped in the southbound lanes; another has one stopped in the northbound lanes. A sheriff's car sits in one of the paths that cross the median. Highway patrol cars sit on the shoulders, one facing each way, ready to roll, to chase, to apprehend if necessary, to ticket. But the second law still applies, so just before this trap I fumble a CD I am trying to put in the player, and my foot comes off the gas. Cruisin', coastin', I smile as I go by.

1:30 p.m. Exit 120 has no services, but it's marked as a chain-up area for trucks. You wouldn't know this road was heading toward the slide and crash of ice by looking at the surrounding hills, more rounded than jagged, covered with trees, sage grasses, hay bales, irrigated fields. To the east though, the mountains rise, now tall enough to break the tree line. As the afternoon progresses, the clouds grow stronger and larger, thicker. I can see the occasional cloudburst falling in the mountains to the east. In a couple miles, i-15 intersects i-70 and I'll be turning east toward the mountains, toward the storms. i-15 climbs, goes through a series of road cuts, twists, crests a small pass. The sign says 5 percent downgrade next two miles. The road descends into yet another mountain valley, hills gently rising on each side. Strong winds buffet the cars and trucks. Like the others behind me now, this valley is more green than brown.

Back in Beaver, a young man walked up to clean the windshield after I started pumping the gas. He complimented the Jeep and we fell to talking. I told him my family had had an old cj-7 for twenty years before I turned it in for this one, and that we'd owned several others before that one too.

"What year?" he asked.

" '83," I said.

"Ah," he said, smiling. "I had an '85. Had to drop a v8 in that one. The old straight six just wasn't enough power for burning up the hills."

I didn't say anything. But I think about him again, north of Beaver, when I see a road sign with just one black word on the yellow sign: Damage.

1:49 in the afternoon. I-15 continues north from here to Salt Lake City, and then farther north into Montana, but I-70 begins here too and heads east toward Richfield and Denver and beyond that to places well known in my own history. Somewhere still in front of me, the hope of Mount Evans and whatever that may bring.

∼

I turn east on I-70. The clouds to the east are still more white than dark, but larger. Textbook pictures of thunderstorms developing. As it leaves I-15, I-70 heads straight for hills. Just rises and foothills now, at least as far as I can see. But there are mountains over the horizon, under those clouds. Mountains in front of me and a sun setting behind me. I may not have enough time.

Denver, the sign says, is 507 miles in front of me. Mount Evans is just this side of Denver. But right now I'm entering the Fish Lake National Forest. Only six miles into I-70 and already the road is climbing. I shift into a lower gear. The vista behind me reveals the size of this valley, the mountain range is in the far west distance. About eight miles in, I crest the first hill and am on a downgrade side, the highway falling into yet another valley, this one green with trees.

A small burned area appears on the south side of the interstate. I know I've already passed fires this day, though none of them visible from the road. I've not looked at the fire maps at all since this morning. Will they be close enough to the road for me to see, for me to smell? Will the smoke slow traffic, stop it altogether, or only register like a passing light perfume behind the smell of sage and desert?

I-70 does not follow a valley here. It heads straight east, cuts across each rise and fall. A sign tells me there is a brake test area in two miles. Although the Jeep is still in sunshine, a cloudburst obscures the top of the mountain to the southeast of me. To the north, the sky is busy with contrails and cumulus. Only twelve miles in and the road is going up again. Again, I've had to shift into a lower gear. In front of me, the brake test area. I'm sure it's a swift rocket ride down into the next valley before rising again.

Six Percent Downgrade, the sign says. Brake Test Area, the sign says.

Speed on by.

Sixteen miles in and the roadside landscape is changing. I'm passing the first runaway lane for trucks that cannot control or stop their downhill need. And the rocks are turning redder again, all weathered and broken. An exit for the Fremont Indian State Park and Museum. Petroglyphs, pottery, arrowheads, and grinding stones. The Five Finger Ridge Village, the largest known Fremont Indian village, unearthed by the I-70 construction and then paved over.

I-70 follows the canyon down the eastern side of a small range, traverses a small valley, begins to rise again. It seems like every mile eastward becomes a little more arid, a little more broken. To the north, red rock becomes almost white then turns brown again.

I pass the town of Elsinore and the desire to stop, to tell the people there that my family was Danish too. The elevation here is 5,335 feet above sea level. My foot, it seems, is very heavy. A cloudburst on the north side of the highway is small but diligent, and in my mind I know there's not enough water in the clouds to cause a problem, but that doesn't stop my imagination from looking into the hills and waiting for the torrent, the rocks and sand and silt rushing across the roadway, sucking us all in like molasses or glue.

The Jeep comes up behind a group of motorcycles. Two dozen, I think, though I don't start counting early enough. All of us speeding east on I-70. Some of the riders wear helmets; some of them do not. One of them wears an old coonskin hat, its tail flapping in the wind.

A short while later, I'm passed by two trucks. The first one has a bumper sticker that says, "Improve the Desert. Eat a Sierra Clubber." The second one has a simpler message. "Sierra Club Sucks." I resist the temptation to drive them both into a ditch.

In the town of Salina, Utah, elevation 5,160 feet, I pull over because the sign on the highway says, "No Gas, No Services for the Next 110 Miles." I'm heading off into the desert; so I think I'll top off the tank. At the gas station, a group of young women, either Amish or Mennonite or Hutterite, the kind who wear little white scarves for hats and long gingham dresses, walk out of the convenience store holding postcards, each of them smiling. There are no horses and buggies at the station, so strict Amish is out, I think. I simply write a question in my notes. And although I do not know this yet, in a few months I will send e-mail to a friend who lives in Salt Lake City and ask her what best guess she has for who these women were. What she will write back to me is: "They might have just been part of some Mormon pioneer reenactment or a family reunion—those aren't uncommon, particularly in the summer months. Or perhaps they were actual Mormon polygamist 'sister-wives' on holi-day from their enclave. Although I'd have trouble imagining sister-wives calling attention to themselves in public in the way you describe, two of the largest openly fundamentalist/polygamist communities are not far south of Salina in Hildale, Utah, and Colorado City, Arizona. The women in those places dress the way you describe—but the hats tend to tip my opinion toward the reenactment/reunion theory."

Stories. And history. Well beyond what I can see from this roadway, well beyond the hints I can capture. A sign says, "Frequent Deer and Elk Crossing Next 7 Miles."

Three o'clock in the afternoon. I-70 comes out of a series of canyons and draws, goes through a ravine, white rock on both sides, and settles into a broad plain. Cliffs are all around. This is postcard Utah: red cliffs, white cliffs, the erosion, the alluvial fans. This is high desert. The clouds are thicker than they were, but I can still see blue sky between them. Two or three isolated cloudbursts mark the eastern distance.

Down through another canyon into a lower plain. White rock be-comes red rock. It's like driving through the bottom of the Grand Can-yon, the layers of sediment visible in the cliff faces. Occasionally, the road comes out of a small canyon and the turn is almost frightening.

No guardrail. For the twenty miles in front of me, all I can see is a broad plain of red slick rock. The road turns to the left, and I'm mostly sure I'll make it. If I don't, I could be launched out into the desert. It's beautiful and terrifying at the same time.

3:40 in the afternoon and the road is wet from a passing cloudburst. The sky to the east appears more clear now than threatening, just one cell remaining to the north, and the air is heavy with the smell of sage. It's a beautiful day in the American desert, at eighty miles an hour, heading west into the Rocky Mountains through the suddenly green and fragrant desert.

More brake test sites, more 6 percent grades. "Sharp Curves." "Steep Grades." It's what I would imagine on Mars.

The sun appears between the clouds to illuminate pockets of the valley I'm driving into. Brilliant reds and then the muted colors where a cloud obscures the sun.

I'm waiting for the car in front of me to explode. The driver's been riding the brakes all the way down the hill. My ears are popping. A runaway truck ramp one mile ahead. Happily, no trucks in the rearview mirror.

In the distance, odd smoke. Fire smoke rising from behind a ridge thirty miles or more away, merging with the smoky color of the clouds.

A 6 percent downgrade. I-70 plummets through a cutout in the rock.

And then the town of Green River, Utah, elevation 4,079 feet. The return of Hardee's and Burger King to the desert. A sign tells me I'm forty miles away from Canyonlands National Park, forty miles away from Arches National Park. But east of town the land flattens out to a series of white-brown mesas. For the first time in the distance, I can see the rise of the western edge of the Rocky Mountains in Colorado.

∾

Cloudburst rain in front of me. Brief but intense. Rain hanging like a hard curtain across the road. I crash into it, through it, and I can feel the press of the water slow the Jeep. Windshield wipers set on high speed. Lightning strikes somewhere near. The sign says, "Only You Can Prevent Forest Fires."

The wind from the north moves the rain across the highway in sheets and waves. I watch as the rain washes the left side of the Jeep clean, while the right side, in the rain shadow, stays caked with road dust. A mile, perhaps a mile and a half, into it, though, I'm through the other side and back on dry asphalt.

A white Toyota pickup truck blasts past me, even though I'm driving eighty miles an hour. Inside the bed of the truck, four young men hunker down against the wind and rain. They all nod and smile, gamely, at me as they pass. To the south, a half dozen dust devils whip up dust from the desert where the rain has yet to arrive. A portable highway sign flashes, "Warning—Dust Storm Area—Use Caution."

5:11 in the afternoon. Three hundred miles from Denver. Four hours left! Will there be any light left in the sky?

Cliffs to my left, dark now under the overcast sky. And here is a story I know. The Book Cliffs, a thousand feet high, two thousand feet high when they join with the Roan Cliffs near Green River, this rise is 250 miles long, the longest continuous escarpment in the world. And according to the notes I carry, 375 vertebrate species move in the scene I'm blurring by. Fifty species of mammals: elk, deer, cougar, bear, bighorn sheep. And underneath it all, oil. Enough oil for companies to tear up the land, to build new roads, to push a permanent value into gravel in favor of a fleeting need. Yes, I'm driving a Jeep that needs oil and gas. There are contradictions in every person's life that cannot be finally resolved. But contradiction does not mean lack of purpose or hope. I oppose these roads with my car, if you will. And in other ways too.

~

5:17 p.m. Welcome to Colorful Colorado!

As I-70 crosses into Colorado, it goes up a small rise and into another valley; leaving a broader flat land behind me. I do not know what surveyors set this boundary or why or when, but the land is different here. I-70 is no longer the flat, straight stretch. Now it winds as the valley rises toward hills and, in the background, mountains. The land is less red rock and hard gravel, more sage and more brown dirt. Pinyon-juniper trees forest both sides of the road.

Colorado is simply different. It is certainly filled with as many as extremes as California, as Nevada, as Utah—extremes in elevation, extremes in distance, extremes in abundance and scarcity, lush with valleys, the ability to steal your breath at every corner of the highway. But the Colorado seen from I-70 heading east here in the evening is a softer beauty, a more substantial beauty, older perhaps. As the highway skirts the outside of the town of Mack, I can see off to the northeast a range of mountains, white cliffs, forests. The valley between them is broad and green with trees and fields, homes. Straight ahead over a ridge of red rock licked by the sun now descending in the sky, a classic thunderhead, anvil-topped and brilliant white. A highway sign says, "Fire Ban in Effect. Extreme Fire Danger."

5:30 p.m. The Colorado River parallels the highway and rafters enjoy a summer afternoon paddle slowly with the current. Grand Junction, elevation 4,600 feet, comes and goes. The sign says, "Gusting Winds Likely Next Four Miles." The town of Palisade, watered by the Colorado, is green and lush with orchards and vineyards: the Grand River Vineyards and Winery. Beyond Palisade, I-70 makes a downhill run into another canyon. I pass an eighteen-wheeler hauling a load of onions.

The river is low and shallow and tumbling over itself. Occasionally, a little spillover dam holds the water back and then erases it. The canyon is sometimes steep and deep enough I can't see over the top. Sometimes, it opens up to the mountains in the distance and trees. There is a railroad line on the north side of the river and the highway on the south. At the top of small rise, a vista opens to the northeast. I write a note to myself—look up the history of the word "majestic."

6:25 and the roadway rises through the Grand Valley toward the towns of Parachute and Rifle. White cliffs on the north. Green forest mountains to the south. The Colorado River meanders through the center of it all. The town of Parachute, elevation 5,095 feet above sea level. Then Battlement Mesa, "one of the most luxurious residential communities in the country." A long way from Badwater, I think. And then the town of Rifle, elevation 5,335 feet.

6:51 in the evening. Still climbing through the Grand Valley. A valley soft in the late summer afternoon sunlight. I don't know if it's still the Colorado River, but the stream that winds through the valley makes everything look green, and as the slopes begin and rise the earth turns brown. In the bottom of the valley, horses graze in green pastures, trees line the waterways. It's a very pretty sight.

The town of Silt, elevation 5,432 feet. Geese spiral downward before landing on water. The sides of the Grand Valley are close up enough now to call this place a canyon instead of a valley. I pass a rafter who has just pulled up to an access and is unloading the raft, and I find myself filled with a familiar envy, perhaps even jealousy. To spend a day at river speed instead of road speed. To do this same dance to that other music. It's the same envy I have of pilots who fly very small airplanes. And the same envy I have for astronauts. I'm never sure if perfection is to be Buddha, to sit and watch the play of geologic time unfold before the unmoving self, or to be Jean-Luc Picard, to wave a hand and firmly command a starship to "engage."

Approaching Canyon Creek, a railway on the north side and a train hauling coal cars. Birds in the stream. The town of Glenwood Springs, elevation 5,746 feet, and the White Water Rafting Company. Exit 116, for Glenwood Springs, is also the exit for Aspen. There are people floating tubes down the waterway, a handful of men in waders fly fishing. In Glenwood Springs, there are gondola ride to the top of the hill even in July. The highway goes through a tunnel.

Exit 119 is for a place called No Name. Perfect, I think. Already there are too many stories here. Very soon I'll be in the landscape of my own history, college trips to Copper Mountain and Breckenridge, desire at the Loveland Pass. And these places are close enough to my own home that I sometimes hear their news. Resource issues in the Front Range. Segments of I-70 that simply fall away and then downhill. What can I say when I am no longer being introduced? The apparent story is no longer the only or the best definition. No Name, I think, is a good place to stretch before the final fast race against the failing light toward a summit and that last illumination.

There are others here at the rest stop. Men and women and children and pets stare at the river, stop by the bathroom, stare at the river, bend and stretch their arms and legs and tails, stare at the river, walk back to their cars and trucks, stare at the river, get in and drive away. A romantic couple at the shelter touch each other, nuzzle and kiss each other, hug and do not mind the people who watch. She laughs loudly when he tickles her.

I stretch, then stare at the river. Patience, it seems, has left me. I have somewhere to be. I have somewhere I need to be, and fast.

There is not enough room in this canyon for the highway, the river, the railway. The westbound side of the highway is elevated, built on concrete pilings and retaining walls. The eastbound side of the highway also built on retaining walls and pilings but lower. Just over the guard-rails, the river. Hard against the water, the rails. And, incredibly, a bike path is squeezed into the mix as well. Rafters and tubers and kayakers even this late in the evening still paddle or float their way down. One woman rides her solitary bicycle uphill.

At the exit for Grizzle Creek the canyon tightens further. Then the exit for Hanging Lake and a sign over the highway says, "Stop. Traffic Ahead." No, I pray. Hanging Lake is a small dam; a reservoir behind it and a tunnel for the highway. No traffic, though. No need to stop. A prayer that is answered.

7:25 in the evening and the valley breaks open into a high valley. The sides no longer steep and imposing, but now gentle, forested, rounded at the top. This section of the highway is maintained by the Colorado Friends of John Denver.

At 7:46 the exit for Steamboat Springs and all I see is an endless stretch of roadway that curves through a gentle valley. The hilltops here are for-ested and grass covered, not the hard peaks of farther east and farther west. Stables are on either side of the highway. Good ones. Expensive looking. Horses in the pastures graze, their tails wiping back and forth.

Coming around a bend, I descend into another steep valley. There are homes on the summits. A bridge crosses the Eagle River. Money, I think. Lots of it.

From the scenic overlook just west of the town of Edwards, I can see cattle grazing in a field, then the river, and then the town, and then a valley, green and rising, that cuts into the granite peaks, snow still hid-ing in the shallow places. Here near the highway, the town has stables, soccer fields, a Sunday night baseball game, a community park.

The town of Avon, elevation 7,430 feet, and the exit for the Beaver Creek ski area. This evening the slopes are green grass, a lighter green than the dark green forest. Avon is immaculate, condos all built in cha-let style. I can imagine this place in winter. There is skiing here and beauty in the hills, and money. I wonder, in summer, though, how many of these condos sit empty.

The National Mining Museum at 7:58 in the evening.

8:15 in the evening, and dusk is settling into the valleys. The highway shoulder widens for another chain-up area, for trucks and heavy snow. I do not know if I will be fast enough! The speed limit slows to thirty-five miles an hour for construction. Traffic moves just below fifty. I don't know if I'll be fast enough to chase the sun back up to 14,000 feet at Mount Evans. I hope to catch the last glimmer.

Still climbing steeply into the mountains. The forests have given over completely to lodgepole pines. I was too slow to get a good look, but there are elk on the westbound pavement. I hope people see them.

The Vail Pass, elevation 10,603 feet. I know I will not catch the sun at the top of Mount Evans. All around me, the granite peaks are in shadow. The sky is still light, and there's the hope that I'll see the last lingerings of this day by the time I reach the top. But the direct rays, the rays I ran from this morning, will be gone.

8:30 p.m. Copper Mountain and Leadville. Then a fast ride down a valley. Darkness comes into the landscape. Everybody's headlights are on. Mountains begin to melt into each other in the darkness. The speed limit is sixty-five again, but we're all doing eighty.

Then the exit for Breckenridge. The road begins to rise again, and then the tunnel for the Loveland Pass, elevation 11,992 feet. The Continental Divide! It's all downhill from here, until that last climb on Mount Evans. The Arapahoe National Forest and the town of Silver Plumb, elevation 9,118 feet. The scenic area comes and goes—darkness having settled into the valley. 6 percent downgrade. Georgetown, elevation 8,519 feet. Pure dark in the canyon now, but the sky above still has the pale blue light of twilight.

Eleven miles from Idaho Springs. Fog has settled over the highway and signs say, "Heavy Traffic. Expect Delays."

9:08 p.m. The traffic slows to fifteen miles an hour on I-70 as we crawl downhill toward Denver. Then ten miles an hour. The sky above me is dark enough now I watch airplane lights head west toward Los Angeles. Then the traffic stops.

9:18 p.m. We're moving again, and even though I am approaching the exit for Idaho Springs, we're moving slowly enough that the woman driving the car next to me is knitting.

Finally! Idaho Springs, elevation 7,540 feet above sea level. 9:34 in the evening. I accelerate on the exit ramp.

In town, I pass a hotel with a No Vacancy sign and get worried. I haven't arranged a place to stay tonight. The sky has gone black, all hope of catching the day's finale gone down too, so I spend a few minutes and find a funky little hotel on the east side of town.

"May be the last bed in town tonight," the clerk tells me.

I smile and thank her, then tell her I'll be back in a few hours. I'm going to drive up to the top of Mount Evans.

"That road's closed," she tells me.

"What?" I ask, incredulous.

"That road closes at sunset."

"No it doesn't."

"Yes it does."

"I called," I say. "I talked to the Park Service. They said it was open twenty-four hours."

"Not that I've ever heard," she says.

But then we leave it at that. She smiles and wishes me luck. Back in the Jeep, fresh gas in the tank, fresh coffee in my cup, I fish in my pack for a guidebook the Park Service ranger sent me some weeks ago. *A Day On Mount Evans: A Guide for Travelers Exploring the Highest Paved Road in North America.* And as tired as I am, I almost weep at the list of things I will not see in the darkness: mule deer, prairie falcon, coyote, chipmunk, Steller's jay, Clark's nutcracker, Albert's squirrel, raven, golden-mantled ground squirrel, chickaree, Rocky Mountain elk, blue grouse, snowshoe hare, gray jay, white-tailed ptarmigan, brown-capped rosy finch, American pipit, yellow-bellied marmot, pika, Rocky Mountain bighorn sheep, mountain goat. I will not see the plants named alpine sunflower, king's crown, harebell, fairy primrose, sly pilot, alpine forget-me-not, little red elephant, Indian paintbrush, Colorado blue columbine, golden banner. And when I get to the summit, I will not see Pike's Peak in the far southern distance. I will not see Rosalie Peak, Epaulet Mountain, Kataka Mountain, Mount Bierstadt, the Mount of the Holy Cross. I will not see the Sangre de Cristo Range, the Sawatch Range, the Mosquito Range, the Gore Range either.

But I will go up this hill nonetheless, and I swear if there is a gate across the road I will crash my way through it.

The Mount Evans road is open. So I begin this last road in a darkness that makes it impossible to tell what I'm passing. Forests of spruce on both sides of the road, the occasional lodge or home, trucks parked in the gravel lot. Above me, the sky is now pitch black, though the stars have come out. The sign says, "Steep Grades, Sharp Curves Next Seven Miles." Another sign tells me I'm back in the Arapahoe National Forest. Then a very small sign says, simply, 8,620. At first I think it's an address. Then I pass another that reads 8,810, and I realize I'm reading elevation.

The roadway beyond the light of my headlights is invisible to me. Overhead, the stars are bright and the sky is clear. Sometimes I can see from what light there is the ridgetops of the ranges around me, but more often from this road a vista opens up and all I can see is the blackness—a blackness that's deep and fat enough to let me know there is tremendous space there, a tremendous hole I can only feel with the hair on the back of my neck. In second gear, I'm traveling twenty-five miles an hour uphill, around hairpin curves and ledges. Even at night, it's an exciting drive.

I pass a sign that reads Devil's Canyon, though no canyon is visible in only starlight. I smile when I read this section of the road is maintained by the Alpine Rescue Team.

10:04 p.m. I'm climbing above a ski station on the road to Mount Evans. The road hugs the cliff face. The Jeep creeps along, barely in second gear. On my left then, suddenly, a huge pool of orange and white light—the whole of Denver spread out in the distance, and distance itself is visible again. I can see how far it is to the city, and I can see the size of the abyss between here an there. "Oh my God!" I say, though no one is around me to hear. The sight is that big.

10:06 p.m. I've climbed above the tree line.

10:12 p.m. It is the end of July, and I'm driving past a snowfield. A sign says, "Road Damage." Some bumps and heaves in the road, and I don't know if they are washouts or frost heaves. They're quickly over.

10:37 p.m. I'm at the top of Mount Evans! The lights of Denver in the eastern distance, the stars above more brilliant than I could ever imagine. I pull the Jeep into a parking spot and shut it off. When the ticking of the cooling engine fades, there is finally no sound at all. Not even wind. I open the door of the Jeep and step out, and my legs are unsturdy beneath me. I laugh, thinking this is only a temporary weak knee, but I feel like I am going to wobble whatever distance I attempt. I'm lightheaded and dizzy from the altitude.

The summit is actually a little bit farther up from here, but the roadway ends. I know there's a hike to the summit, to the University of Denver observatory, where there may be someone even tonight focusing that telescope on some other faraway hope, but it's not one I'm going to take in the dark. I had hoped to get here while there was some light left in the sky, though right now I feel blessed by the delays. Here, with the universe above me, what I hear are the names we have given to the places we can only visit in mathematics and imagination. Sagittarius, the archer. Scorpius, the scorpion, with Antares, the red giant star, in its belly. Hercules, Pegasus, Cassiopeia, Ursa Major and Ursa Minor, Polaris and Vega.

I began this day in a valley, the light from our own star chasing me up a hill and onto a roadway. And I end this day under the light of a galaxy. So many stories, so many sights, so much history and so much future in between. There is a kind of grace in the ability to see both in a single day.

I find a rock, then lay down upon it. I could spend the night here, I think, happily watching the stars spin their slow circle above me. But there are people who are waiting to hear my voice tonight, people who are waiting to hear even this first blush at the story of one day's trip. It's time to drive back down the mountain.

Tonight, telephone and sleep. Tomorrow, my Jeep will find the prairie and I will drive toward home.

The Road in Winter

Day One: Moorhead, Minnesota, to Miles City, Montana

Eleven o'clock on a brilliant and cloudless Wednesday morning, after a sunrise with sundogs—three suns rising in the frozen eastern sky—and I'm heading west on I-94 into the prairie of North Dakota. Towns named Fargo, Wheatland, Absaraka, and Casselton have already faded in the rearview mirror. Ahead of me, the hard light of sunshine on flatland snowfields. Then foothills. Then mountains.

When I left this morning, the temperature was 13 degrees below zero—30 degrees below zero on the revised wind chill scale. It was 18 below in Crookston, 17 below in Jamestown. The National Weather Service office in Grand Forks has issued a wind chill advisory, but the radar is clear. The forecast in Fargo is minus 9 at noon—minus 19 tonight. In the forecast, there is snow in the mountains and colder air to the west.

Like most road trips, this one began a long time ago. An invitation came from friends in Spokane. "Come visit," they said, "Do some work out here; see what it's like." Dates were arranged, the road atlas checked. Easy enough, I thought. A straight shot west. Several days ago, however, the weather maps became more important—the maps that showed the cold to come and the snow moving in. The road in winter, the highways of the northern prairie that race west and then rise into the mountain passes, is often beautiful and often lethal. On the evening news we hear stories of the lost, the stuck, the frozen, and the dead. Then over coffee we hear stories of hoarfrost in the trees, or fields of snow shaped by wind to look like the swells of a gentle ocean, or a shimmering world where ice simply floats in the air. I could see this, I thought. I could see this on purpose, and not just as sidelight to some other errand.

It would be wrong to say this morning is anything less than beautiful. The flatland of the prairie, land that in summer springs wheat and sugar beets and soybeans as quickly as softball and soccer teams, trips to the lakes for walleye and bass, swimming and rest, is today covered with fresh snow on a layer of ice. The fields are motionless and white, but easily bring to mind a bay or harbor, a storm approaching but not yet seen, the waves just beginning to rise. The trees and fence lines look like holiday ornaments. The prairie in hard winter reaches the same places within us as any iceberg, any glacier, any picture of Europa or Neptune. But with beauty there is always an edge. And winter is the season of the very, very cold.

I am heading west in a twenty-year-old Jeep with a soft top. The Jeep is in good mechanical condition, but the body needs restoration. As I look past my left knee, I can see the pavement through the floor. If I lift the carpet, a larger hole is revealed. Air seeps in around the doors, through the soft top, in the back window, and through the floor. It's 13 degrees below zero outside. The air coming in through the floor is slower than the speed of the Jeep, but still a bullet to my legs and feet. At fifty miles an hour, the wind chill would be minus 50 on the new scale, minus 75 on the old. The thermometer hanging from my coat says it's less than 50 inside, and the heater is on full fan.

This trip, I think, is a wonderful idea. Wearing thermal boots, long underwear, jeans, a fleece sweatshirt, a coat that would have impressed Robert Falcon Scott, chopper mittens, a hat, and glacier glasses, I am not cold but it is cold outside. Were the Jeep to stop, however, the engine to die, I could be in trouble.

∽

The traffic this morning seems more like mirage than reality. There is a mile between me and the truck in front of me, another mile between me and the truck behind. On the eastbound lanes, five or ten minutes go by before an eighteen-wheeler passes, and then another quiet.

The rivers are frozen, as are the bridges that cross them. Each "Watch for Ice" sign more than a simple suggestion. In the distance, what looks like a fog is really snow raised by the wind. Outside the town of Ayr, cattle graze at their delivered food near a farmstead. The prairie does look like an ocean in winter—waves whipped up in the snow, crests, small cornices hanging from each one. An ambulance, lights flashing, passes on the eastbound lanes.

It would be easy to say the prairie in winter is a desolate place, a lonely place. And this would be close to true if all you considered was the visible. Yet, I know this is not true. While it is too cold and the frost in the ground is too deep for anyone to work this land today, acre after acre of farmland here is being readied in the minds of the farmers, in the bank accounts, and in the grocery stores. Machinery is being repaired, seeds are being ordered, snow is being measured for water content. In every farmhouse, hopes for the future are measured against stories of the past.

I can see my breath inside the car.

⁓

Sometimes in failure, there is a hidden grace. My radio does not work. My CB radio, which worked just fine yesterday, does not work this morning. So, I cannot hear the songs or the news of the outside world. What I am asked to pay attention to is the sound of my car, the soft top rattling like gravel and occasionally snapping like gunshot. And also another kind of silence—the silence of the landscape, the trees, the snowpack, the cold, the ice crystals hanging in the air.

I pass the exit for the towns of Buffalo and Alice. I pass a road-killed deer. Earlier a pure white farm turkey, frozen, fluttered on the shoulder, blown off its truck by who knows what gust or accident.

More than one thousand planes will cross the state this day. Planes from Japan heading for Minneapolis. Commuter flights. Planes with student pilots. More than 150 radio and television stations fill the air with news and music, comedy and drama from someplace warmer. Tens, perhaps hundreds, of thousands of cars and trucks will move something or someone from one place to another. E-mail erupts from every possible outlet. Stores are open. Banks are open. Everything is open. Electricity arrives from everywhere. Furnaces burn natural gas delivered by pipeline from Canada. Coal is lifted from the earth and loaded on trains. In almost every way it is possible to ignore the cold, the wind, the taste of the unheated air. It is almost possible to ignore the whole outside.

On the east side of Valley City, a wind turbine generator I've never seen before rises off the south side of the interstate. According to the thermometer on my coat, the temperature inside the Jeep has fallen below 40 degrees.

In Valley City, the hills are soft and white, snow-covered, like cotton. Brown oak and elm trees, green pines come up out of the snow. There's not much traffic on the roads in town, even less on the highway. A truck behind me exits; nothing replaces him. West of town, the snow up against the highway fences rises like breakers on a beach.

~

If summertime on the American prairie is filled with optimism, with springtime rain, summer planting, and then the green of midsummer crops, the gold of harvesttime, red combines moving through yellow fields of wheat, if all of that speaks to promise and prosperity, to health and the American dream, what is it our imagination says about the snow-covered and frozen prairie in January when the temperature is many degrees below zero?

We tell stories about the Dakota winter. We use words like blizzard, storm, wind chill. I once asked my friend John Wheeler, a meteorologist, what was the worst blizzard in North Dakota history. He said that was a matter of some contention—different parts of the state have different answers. But January 11–13, he said, in 1888, was a pretty good bet.

On the morning of January 11, the first day of the blizzard, the temperature was 44 degrees below zero. The day warmed considerably, all the way up to minus 4, and then it began to snow. There was already more than a foot of snow on the ground, and with the snow came the wind. All the Department of Commerce records say is that there were gale force winds, thousands of cattle frozen, loss of life was great. But that is enough to imagine the storm. On January 12 the temperature rose to 12 degrees above zero and most of the snow fell. Then day turned to night and the temperature fell. 28 degrees below zero on the thirteenth. A high temperature of minus 25 on the fourteenth. Brutally cold, John said. And I agreed.

Later, I discovered this entry on the Web, attributed to the *Encyclopaedia Britannica* of 1893:

> In one [blizzard] which visited Dakota and the States of Montana, Minnesota, Nebraska, Kansas and Texas in January, 1888, the mercury fell within twenty-four hours from 74° above zero to 28° below it in some places, and in Dakota went down to 40° below zero. In fine clear weather, with little or no warning, the sky darkened and the air was filled with snow, or ice-dust, as fine as flour, driven before a wind so furious and roaring that men's voices were inaudible at a distance of six feet. Men in the fields and children on their way from school died ere they could reach shelter; some of them having been not frozen, but suffocated from the impossibility of breathing the blizzard. Some 235 persons lost their lives. This was the worst storm since 1864; the Colorado River in Texas was frozen with ice a foot thick, for the first time in the memory of man.

Ranchers, John said, might say the blizzard of January 28–29 a year earlier, in 1887, was worse, since more snow fell in the western part of the state. (And a famous blizzard, killing more than four hundred people and changing nearly everything we do concerning warnings, hit New York City, Washington DC, and New England March 11–14 in 1888.) Even in my own history, the blizzards of 1997 brought four storms in January and left me and my family stranded on the highways of South Dakota, unable to see the road in front of us, no place to stay, unable to move.

All of this is possible, as is the farmhouse window I see suddenly catch the light of the sun and reflect it back, turning the home for one brief instant into a star on the sunlit ground. The road in winter is nothing if not the home of the unexpected and the possible. In front of me still, the Badlands, the Montana prairie, then the mountains. More snow. More cold. And it would be wrong to say this morning is anything less than beautiful.

~

Approaching Jamestown, out of habit I look for the bison herd that lives at the feet of the giant roadside fiberglass bison statue. Not a single animal seems present. Rounding a curve I look back over my shoulder and see them standing in a hollow out of the wind.

In Jamestown, I stop at Wal-Mart because my feet have been freezing, and I buy heated pads to go inside my boots. That brief stop, however, is a shock. Stepping inside the mall, I'm hit with the return of canned music, televisions, radios, people eating large pizzas. The heat feels good, but the rest of it nearly makes me sick. In the parking lot, a dozen cars all run unattended, smoke billowing from their exhaust pipes. The temperature is 10 degrees below zero. A strong cup of coffee from a fast-food place, and I'm back on the road.

It is difficult but important to remember how nonlocal is most of what sustains us. And how ignorant we are of the origins. The cows that gave their lives for the hamburger I ate this morning could have been raised outside of Moorhead or outside of Tallahassee. The fish that gave its life to become my lunch at McDonald's never swam in local water. The wintergreen candy I just popped into my mouth was, for all I know, made on Mars. This coffee is not from North Dakota.

Chemicals warming my toes, as the Jeep comes back up to highway speed I find myself wondering about the yellow barrels placed at the posts and supports for bridges where the interstate crosses under county roads. Highway Department crash barriers, essentially large buckets filled with water, meant to disperse the energy of a car crashing into the bridge. When the temperature is 10, 15, 20 degrees below zero though, I wonder if those buckets are frozen and, if a crash were to happen, would they send a shower of splintering ice into the air, each fleck a possible rainbow? Farther on, I see how occasionally tracks leave the highway, cross the median or dead-end in a ditch. Stories from yesterday or the day before.

∾

In Bismarck the temperature is still 6 degrees below zero. As I cross the Missouri River, an odd area of open water steams, otherwise the ice is broken only by pressure and by wind sculpting the snow. Along the river, Lewis and Clark, just north of here, wintered near the Mandan village. In this sense "to winter" is a verb, an action word that means "to stay put."

In the Lewis and Clark journals from January 1804 we read:

Ice thick, wind hard.... Wind blew excessively hard ... a cold day ... a verry Cold clear day, the Themtr Stood at 22 d below 0 wind.... This morning a boy of 13 years of age Came to the fort with his feet frozed, haveing Stayed out all night without fire, with no other Covering than a Small Robe goat skin leagens & a pr. Buffalo Skin mockersons—the Murcery Stood at 72 below the freesing point—Several others Stayed out all night not in the least hurt, This boy lost his toes only . . . a verry Cold Day. . . . Observed an Eclips of the Moon.

To winter, or, in more common use now, to winter over, is a smart thing to do. The races to the arctic and antarctic poles have included whole seasons of waiting, of patience, of hope and humility. To move in winter is frankly a new idea.

At a gas station here in Bismarck, another Jeep driver walks up, smiles, says, "I like the fly in your window." I have a fishing fly a friend gave me hanging from the rearview mirror. A pickup truck driver filling up next to me points to the Jeep and says, "Those things heat up pretty good in the winter?" I tell him it does in spite of the fact that today I am freezing. He smiles and nods, says, "I've always wanted one of those."

I tell the gas station clerk I am driving west and hope to make Billings tonight but will probably only make Miles City. He shakes his head and says, "Between here and Billings, it's just one long, boring drive."

I nod in complete disagreement. His drive, I am sure, is one long loud radio song and an urge to get there. On the road, I rise to a hilltop west of town and see the landscape change the way it does in North Dakota west of the Missouri River. Suddenly there are hills and rises, valleys and ravines. A tumbleweed manages to jump the highway fence and hits my door and window dead-on, where it remains pressed long enough for me to look into its branches before the wind sends it off again. Pretty soon there will be buttes and then the Badlands. Even in winter, with everything snow covered and frozen, with the air itself capable of killing you within a few minutes if you're insufficiently prepared, this is anything but a long, boring drive.

Part of the world is cold; part of the world is warm. Our imagination rests on the warmth in the ease and the comfort, but oftentimes it's the cold that will get us.

⌖

West of Bismarck, the men driving pickup trucks wear cowboy hats. Their trucks are brand new. Nearly all of them are talking on cell phones.

Two semis pass each other, one heading east, one heading west. One from the Bakersville Casket Company. One from Tombstone Pizza.

Exit 72 is the exit for Gladstone and the beginning of the Enchanted Highway, thirty-two miles on the road down to Regent of what claims to be the world's largest metal sculptures. "Geese in Flight" sits just off the interstate. Forty, maybe fifty feet high, huge steel silhouettes of geese welded to rays of a steel sun setting over the Badlands buttes. The Jeep never slows.

Just on the west side of Dickinson, however, one, two, and then four pheasants fly across the road and into a hollow on the northern side. It's 4:30 p.m. mountain time, and the sun is already setting behind the buttes and hilltops. Smoke rises from farmhouse chimneys. The lifting and dipping pumps at the tops of oil wells turn slowly or stand still. Snow covers the hills, the grasslands, and the hollows. Occasionally, I can see cattle bunched around a feeder.

With the setting sun, the road ahead shimmers as if reflecting summer heat, and I almost expect a mirage to rise out of it. But this is not summer heat, and the problem will not be black asphalt melting. This is January in the northern prairie, and black ice, which you can't see on the road at night, can send you suddenly into the ditch, down a cliff, or into something completely different.

The last glimmers of an orange, red, and yellow sunset hold over the Badlands of North Dakota. At the Painted Canyon overlook, an exit with a view into Theodore Roosevelt National Park, the golds and browns and greens of the valleys and rises are covered in snow and made black-and-white, as stark and surprising as a photograph by Ansel Adams, yet there's this surreal sunset above it and to the sides. Every landscape, even the most familiar one, holds the promise of unexpected light. I've been in the Badlands many times, but this picture is a world I've never seen.

~

After stopping for gas at a Flying J travel plaza in Beach, North Dakota, I drive west and quickly find myself in Montana and in darkness. Shortly after the border, a train track approaches and then parallels the south side of the interstate. A train hauling a mile or so of boxcars and oil tanks runs west with me. From the cab of the engine, a small glow, orange and warm, makes me wonder what the engineers think of as they cross the cold northern prairie in night. Do they think of the cars behind them, the goods they are delivering, the people and economies they support? Or are they instead listening perhaps to Joni Mitchell ("Lift me, won't you lift me, beyond the old routine . . ."). Maybe they're listening to Mozart, or reading Melville. Perhaps they are writing a letter to a daughter or a son or a wife or a lover left behind. Maybe they are doing nothing so romantic or noble at all. Maybe they are simply staring forward into the darkness, waiting for the next crossing and the need to sound their horn. It's impossible to tell. I honk the Jeep's feeble horn, hoping for a reply. But there is no way they can hear me.

All through the Badlands, what began as a small tingling in the back of my neck becomes stronger, and there is no way to say it other than to admit I am afraid. Snow is creeping into the passing lane. The road is imperfectly plowed. As I drive, I keep waiting for that telltale slip, a bit of gas given with the accelerator pressed at the wrong time and suddenly the back end is swinging around and I'm facing the wrong direction. Or worse yet, the Jeep begins to slide and suddenly we're catapulted end over end or rolling over. Only a year ago, on a winter's night much warmer than this one, my friend Brian Cole rolled his Jeep on some black ice in Minnesota. "Three times around and three times over," he said, "every window broken out." He walked away and bought a larger car.

Cold, tired, worried, at some point I look out the window and up into the sky. What I expect is nothing—the gray nothing of clouds closing in, heavy with snow and ice. What I see is something else. Clear sky, no moon, and the whole universe of stars, each one distinct and bright, brilliant, cold and hard in the frozen air. Billions of them. A sense of proportion and size visits the westbound highway.

In Dickinson, North Dakota, I stopped at a mall and bought a pair of boots rated to 50 degrees below zero. For the past few hours I have been thinking this road trip may be a dumb idea. Not only dumb but stupid. The thermometer on my jacket says 40 degrees, but I don't believe it. It's said 40 degrees for the past three hours. Even in the new boots my feet are freezing. As I drive farther into the darkness of Montana, I am concerned by what I cannot see and what I can feel. In the darkness, what I cannot see is the land around me. I cannot see the Yellowstone

River when I cross it twice. I cannot see the land, cannot tell if it's hilly or flat. But what I feel is the cold. I have discovered that my head is slowing inching closer to my shoulders. My neck is scrunched over as if I am trying to swallow myself. Both hands are on the wheel. My arms are tight and fists clenched. This is white-knuckle driving, not only because of the ice on the road but because I'm so cold. I am seriously afraid of frostbite on my toes. As the evening grows darker and the night grows longer, the cold grows deeper—10 degrees below zero, 15 below.

At Miles City, I exit and find a hotel. The temperature is minus 16. On the floor of the Jeep, I imagine the temperature is zero at best. The carpet is brittle and ice covered. The heater still pumps warm air—it just can't keep up. The desk clerk looks at my Jeep, then at me, and says anyone who can drive this cold in a soft top needs a discount.

As I haul my one bag into the hotel, I look at the other cars in the lot, the one or two passing on the road. Sealed tightly in cars with efficient heaters, listening to the radio or talking on the phone, it's possible for drivers to have no good idea where they are. I cannot say I am more comfortable. But I am grateful for my discomfort in that discomfort can bring awareness.

There is a part of me that says I didn't have to do this. I could have flown, could have been warm. But the larger part of me knows that had I flown I would have seen nothing real. Perhaps this is a dumb idea. To drive in winter, you need the heat. But to be without it, to be at risk, is something too.

The forecast for tomorrow predicts one to three inches of snow between here and the mountains, three to six inches in the mountains. And cold, the TV says. Hard cold.

Day Two: Miles City, Montana, to Spokane, Washington

At five o'clock when the hotel phone rings, inexplicably, I get up, answer it, and there's no one there. I turn and look out the window. It is still dark but clear and cold. At six o'clock, when the phone rings with my wakeup call, I get up and look out the window again and discover it is snowing and snowing hard. This is a dumb idea.

The temperature, however, is 3 degrees above zero. The forecast high for today is 18. Both numbers make me surprisingly happy. The woman on television still says one to three inches of snow here today, which isn't so bad if the roads stay clear. More snow in the mountains. It's time to get moving.

At the front desk, I ask the desk clerk about the forecast. He says, "You might run into some snow." I tell him I have to make Spokane tonight. "Good luck," he says. I try to pay for the phone bill but the clerk says, "Ah, it's not worth it. Get on the road. Have fun." There's something in his tone of voice that makes me worried.

Strong coffee in the cup, two rolls from the hotel's breakfast on the seat next to me. The heater on full, for what it's worth. The carpet still frozen. Back up to speed on the interstate. Of the two lanes heading west, the left lane is ice covered and snow packed, while loose snow swirls in the right. What looks like a patch of ice suddenly dissolves in the dry pavement. Dry pavement changes to black ice. I've already passed an abandoned U-Haul truck on the right side of the road. It's a difficult morning, but we're all creeping along at fifty miles an hour. Snow blows into the cab of the Jeep, lands on the passenger seat, and does not melt.

By 8:30 the day has dawned into an overcast gray-blue sky. The snow comes and goes, sometimes heavy, sometimes nothing at all. The snow clouds kicked up by passing trucks and cars are substantial. Just before a rest stop, freezing rain falls as if somebody had dumped a bucket. It has the consistency of glue and binds to the wheels and windshield. The car is encased in ice, and the front windshield is about as transparent as a plastic milk jug. Looking through a hole about an inch or maybe two inches across, the full ability of my defroster this morning, I steer to a rest stop, where I spend five minutes with my windshield scraper.

Still east of Billings, the land rolls, and hills covered with pine trees open to pastureland. One farmer with a tractor lifts hay bales onto a truck, but otherwise the fields are empty. The occasional herd of cows appears, hunkered down against the wind.

The freezing rain continues and every car is in trouble. I pull to the side of the road, and as I work to clear the glass I'm passed by a pickup pulling a horse trailer. When I get going, I pass this truck during his turn to scrape. When I pull over again, he passes me. At some point I honk as I pass. He honks when he passes. When I pass him again—two honks. He gives me two on his turn. Three honks. We're laughing at this, waving at each other. Four honks. When he passes me this time, I notice that a sheet of plastic he had taped over the open back of the trailer—I assume to shield his horse's rump from the ice and spray—has blown off. I give him five honks on my turn and never see him again.

At the border of Yellowstone County, a pheasant stands on the side of the road and watches the Jeep approach. It stands there like a statue, intent. When I'm ten to fifteen feet away, suddenly it takes to the air. Three flaps of its wings, and I'm sure I'm going to kill it. Then it swerves, and we don't meet.

∼

9:15 in the morning and I am at the exit for Pompey's Pillar National Landmark, a short distance from the Yellowstone River and William Clark's signature under glass. On the trip back from the Pacific, having separated from Lewis, Clark was impressed by this rock. His engraving is the only evidence of the expedition left on the trail. In the journals he wrote, "Arrived at a remarkable rock situated in an extensive bottom . . . this rock I ascended and from it's top had a most extensive view in every direction. This rock which I shall call Pompy's Tower is 200 feet high and 400 paces in secumpherance and only axcessable on one Side. . . . The nativs have ingraved on the face of this rock the figures of animals & near which I marked my name and the day of the month & year."

Thinking of the Corps of Discovery, one of the things I find necessary to imagine is traveling this country at a different speed. At sixty-five, seventy, or seventy-five miles an hour, the Montana prairie seems endless and, in wintertime, forbidding. To travel this on horseback or on foot or by canoe, to travel at a much slower speed, would lead to a much greater intimacy with the landscape. It would turn my two-day trip into months or a year. But I would not be traveling in winter. And in fact, I would not be making this trip at all.

I sometimes wonder if Jeep speed isn't too fast, if the trip isn't somehow less because of the engine that pulls me toward the mountains. Perhaps. But if this is true, then horse speed is less honest than walking. If the goal is to learn the local world, then any movement is away from perception. If the goal is to see a bit of the whole world, then speed, to a point, is a grace.

To travel at foot speed or canoe speed is to say, "What is this thing here?" To travel at car speed is to say, "What is that thing I see coming?" It's a different way of perceiving where you are.

Just east of Billings, the sun comes out through the overcast sky and the snowfields light up brilliantly. In the distance, I can see the white peaks of what appear to be mountains.

Steam rises straight up from oil and gas refineries on the east side of Billings. No wind. A cold, clear, crystalline day.

As I cross the Yellowstone River Bridge, I see open water. I don't know if it's from the work of the refineries or the river itself. The smell of the refineries hangs thick in the air.

What do we mean when we call a landscape beautiful? West of Billings, the highway goes through small passes in the mountains, pine trees sticking up through white snow, the occasional red barn nestled in a valley. This is certainly a beautiful landscape, but it is not the same kind of a beauty as a rain forest, the slick rock of Utah, a Kansas wheat field, the Everglades, a volcano. I'm beginning to believe there is something hiding in our notions of beauty that is related to health, and something that's related to the mysterious, even perhaps a threat.

At Reed Point there is a clear, sunny sky to the left and a snow squall moving in from the right. A rainbow hangs in the air on the north side of the highway. The passing lane on the westbound track remains snow covered and ice choked. The right lane glistens with moisture where cars have worn the snow and ice to water, but it's liable to freeze at any time. A thin line of snow runs down the middle of the right lane. This is a dangerous road with the weather closing in.

Twice now the Jeep has hit a patch of ice. For a moment I've been convinced I'd soon be on my side. Once going under a bridge and once going over, momentum suddenly shifted and the world was a bit fresher.

A sign points to the Absaroka Range, but I can't see it through the fog. Earlier a sign pointed to the Bear Tooth Range. Although I was in the clear, the peaks were shrouded in mist. It's turning into another hard day on the northern road.

On the east side of Livingston, the wind comes up fast and hard. The road is wet and icy. I pull over to put the Jeep in four-wheel drive. My stomach is in knots. An electronic road sign outside Livingston says,

"Caution—Icy and Snow-Packed Conditions Ahead. Watch for Snow-plows Either Side of the Road." This is a dumb idea.

At a Conoco station, I walk through puddles of water, deep piles of slush. I'm told that the road west is pretty bad, but then a guy comes and says, "No, just up near Bozeman at the top of the pass. It's pretty bad up there."

To the north there is still clear sky and, to the south, gray gunmetal clouds make it impossible to see the mountains other than those close to the roadway. I'm heading west and up, in four-wheel drive on ice and snow. At the gas station I bought a new bottle of windshield washer fluid. The woman said that with a fresh bottle and four-wheel drive, I should be okay. I told her I'd remind myself of that when I wound up upside down. I should be okay.

Twenty-one miles to Bozeman and the pass and where I'm told the road will be at its worst. For what it's worth, though, on the west side of Livingston the sun comes out for just a moment. The Paradise Valley appears like Brigadoon and then closes again in the mist. The world is a breathtaking place. For a mile or so, I can see grass on the highway's shoulders.

∼

The plows have been out and spreading gravel. The few semis that pass me raise plumes and sprays of water, snow, slush, and rock. I'm grateful for every ping against the windshield. Traction. I'm grateful there are no trucks in either of the chain-up areas west of Livingston. Nobody, as far as I can tell, is preparing for a road that bad.

The highway climbs into the mountains, falls into valleys, then climbs again. Heading down one hill, a FedEx double tandem truck does its best to push me faster down the road. Its grille is all I can see in my rearview mirror. Slush and ice are all I can see in front of me. If I start to spin, I think, this truck will be the first thing I hit or that hits me. Then the guardrail. Then the openness of free fall. I'm sure the scenery on either side of the road is wonderful.

In Bozeman the streets are only wet, giant snow piles pushed onto roadway shoulders and corners of parking lots, and I find a moment to breathe again. The temperature is just above freezing. Clear sky to the north and west. A thin fog to the south. Wonderful mountains! Another

44

gas station, and another bottle of windshield washer fluid. The pump at the bottom of the fluid reservoir is leaking.

Two o'clock in the afternoon and I'm passing the exit for the Madison Buffalo Jump State Park. A limestone cliff there, where first peoples dressed as wolves or antelope stampeded buffalo over the cliff to their deaths. Then they collected the meat and hides and bones.

A few minutes later, Three Forks, Montana, and the Missouri Headwaters State Park. The place where Sakakawea was kidnapped by the Hidatsas and taken to Mandan. Five years later, she stood here with Lewis and Clark. The place where John Colter, who remained behind when the Corps moved through on their return, was captured by Blackfeet, stripped naked, and given a head start to run for his life. To everyone's surprise, he ran very fast.

Then Lewis and Clark Caverns State Park. "Perhaps the most popular state park in Montana!" Completely missed by the Corps of Discovery.

Even though the road is dry and clear, I pass two large snowplows coming onto the road and then a spot for chaining up tires. Shortly after that, a sign says, "Icy Spots." The temperature has fallen below freezing again, and in the shadow cast by rock outcroppings and trees the melting snow suddenly freezes. A moment's inattention could be fatal. It's a beautiful landscape. Forested hills. Breaks in the clouds to show snow-capped peaks. An earth with some size and some weight.

Three o'clock in the afternoon and the Continental Divide at 6,393 feet. West of Butte now and passing mountains, dark forests, fields, bright sunshine, little cotton-ball clouds. This trip is a wonderful idea! The Jeep finds a dry groove in the roadway, and I have time to watch the wind blow snow plumes from every summit. Here, I think, is a kind of happiness. Here, I think, is a kind of peace. Watching a landscape unfold, just riding through it for hours or days, without hope or expectation other than the chance to see. In a landscape like this, where every mountain promises another side and a valley, the mystery and reverie are as close and as beyond language as a lover's touch.

Then exit 208 for the towns of Anaconda and Opportunity. Just behind me, I remember, is the Berkeley Pit. One of the most toxic mining sites in the country.

There is something about the imagination that suggests action.

Whispers possibilities. Offers a goal. I pass a small stream to the right of the highway, and my mind leaps to a desire for my fly rod and the act of chasing fish. On the south side of the highway, foothills and then a mountain range, valleys, and peaks make me wonder what it would be like to go there, to climb, to walk there. Something about desire requires us to act. Just as this road, as it travels westward, requires me to find out where it goes.

Wondering, lost in these thoughts, I come around a bend, and for the very briefest of moments I'm convinced that in a field off to the north I see a small, somewhat misshapen elephant. Its head is lowered. Its trunk swings gently.

Of course, this is not an elephant. This is a cow. Just one cow, standing with its back to me. Its tail I mistook for a trunk. When my embarrassment fades, I do begin to wonder what it would be like if we had the mastodons and mammoths back. But I also sit a bit straighter and try to pay a bit more attention.

～

In Drummond I stop for gas and there is a large sign in the window that says, "We support the timber industry." The woman at the register says the roads west are fine but there's supposed to be freezing rain tonight. "Get where you're going before dark," she says. I say, "I'm going to Spokane." She says, "Well, you won't make it." The temperature is 7 degrees above zero.

Freezing rain, more ice on the road. What a wonderful idea! At the exit for Rock Creek Road, I discover I'm in the Sapphire Mountains.

In Missoula, the Bitterroot Mountains to the west are silhouetted by the setting sun. Huge and tremendous; somewhere up there is Lolo Pass, a place I've been before, a place I'd like to see again. The Lolo River. The Lochsa River. The Clearwater River valley. The hardest part of the trip for Lewis and Clark. In the journals they record the high altitude, snow, bad footing for animals and people, fully loaded pack horses rolling down valley sides, lack of food, desperation. Still, what makes the landscape hard also makes it beautiful.

Nighttime comes into the mountains again and fog settles into the valleys. The melting snow on the roadway begins to turn to ice. Near the town of St. Regis, the road goes into a series of twists and turns, and signs advise truckers not to exceed forty-five miles an hour. With the Jeep in four-wheel drive, I'm waiting for that first patch of ice to send me spinning round and round, but it never comes.

The lingering light in the sky is blocked by the earth. Clouds move across the foreclosed skyscapes. Occasionally I pass a bar or a café off to the side and I can see people gathering for dinner, a drink, or just not to be alone.

A sign across the top of the interstate by the town of Haugen, exit 16 in Montana, tells me to watch for icy conditions. Lookout Pass, elevation 4,700 feet, goes under my tires in the darkness.

At a historical marker just over the Idaho border, I stop to figure out why I have no light coming from my headlights. I find the lights, as well as the grille and fenders, encrusted with road grime and ice. Where the ice has melted from the heat of the headlamps, it's run down the grille and frozen. With the round lights, it looks as if my Jeep has been crying. I grab a handful of snow from the roadside and clean the driving lights. When I take another handful to the fog lights, the cold of the snow meets the heat of the lamp and the glass pops as it cracks and splinters. That, I say to myself, was not a good idea.

6 percent downgrade after Lookout Pass. A pull-out area for truckers to check their brakes, runaway lanes for those who check and discover they're in trouble, icy and winding roads leading down out of the pass. The wheel wells of the Jeep eject clouds of spray that bend back to the windows. I do not know the temperature, but I'm squinting again, my head lowering on my neck. In a snowfall, my lights, already dimming, give the effect of driving into a dark tunnel.

I pull off into the town of Kellogg, Idaho, because I can't see. Both the driver's and the passenger's side windows are thick with grime. My windshield wipers are losing the battle and I am again out of washer fluid. No useful light comes from the headlamps or fog lamps. Every truck splashes gallons of hard road muck. When I roll down my window at an intersection to watch for traffic, I honestly cannot believe what I see. There is no snow! It's all gone!

At a gas station, I put the nozzle into the Jeep and turn to look at the man filling the car next to me. I'm wearing my boots that are good to 50 below. He's wearing shorts. And sandals. When I'm back on the highway, a malfunctioning sign at a truck stop tells me the temperature is 150 degrees.

The darkness in the mountains is hard and complete without the moon, but as I crest a small rise and head toward Coeur d'Alene, on the west side of the valley I see what looks like a string of pearls in the sky. Somewhere inside, my mind knows these are the lights of a ski slope, snow machines furiously churning out powder in what is now the temperate air. But from the road I don't have to believe in what they are. Across the distance, they are simply very pretty. A car on some distant frontage road, its lights shining at me, appears to be flying.

In January, I cross the Fourth of July Pass at seventy miles an hour and descend into Spokane, where tomorrow I'll meet my friends and tell them this road story. This evening, though, the pavement is clear. Light rain sometimes falls, and clouds make the stars invisible. But the windows are down in the Jeep and the fresh air feels very good. Later tonight, safe in a hotel room, I will watch a woman on the Weather Channel tell me about the winter storm warning for nearly all of Montana and North Dakota. "If you're planning on traveling in this area," she says, "you might want to reconsider."

Not a chance, I think. This is a wonderful idea.

Mids

Mid-July! Midday! Mid-USA!

One o'clock in the afternoon, mountain time, and I'm on U.S. 85 heading south out of Belfield, North Dakota. The sky overhead is clear, with bright sun, and on both sides of the road the western prairie landscape—the hills and draws and buttes and ravines—spreads out the brown and green and gold light. To the east, a receding cloud drops rain, lightning, and hail on the city of Bismarck. And in the rearview mirror, I can see another storm cell building to the north, though I am sure it will miss me too. The radio, set on scan, brings me Deep Purple's "My Woman from Tokyo," a Brahms concerto, and some country dance song called "The Next Big Thing."

90 degrees in Belfield this afternoon, with the promise of the temperature's climbing. At the Conoco station, just off the exit of I-94, two large women behind the counter entertain the customers. They laugh loudly at everything, a full, rich sound. A customer fumbles some change. "Honey, you want me to hold your hand while I do this?" one of them asks.

The other woman tells stories about something that happened somewhere in town sometime last night. Two couples, husbands and wives, their motorcycles cooling by the front door, pace in aimless circles between the magazine rack and the bathroom—stretching their legs before they're back on the road. A line forms outside the men's bathroom, as somebody's taking far too long. "Don't worry boys," one of the women says. "Nobody's died in there yet."

South of town the wheat fields are still green though hints of brown are just beginning to appear. Farmers have mowed the road's shoulders, leaving long swaths of grass. Already hay ricks can be seen up and down the road, waiting for the farmers to come back with forklifts and trucks to lift and then cart the feed away. Black-and-white cattle crowd together near some water in a small ravine.

~

This is Highway 85, heading south through the western prairie, through the Badlands, the Black Hills, the Custer National Forest, the geographical center of the United States. This is summertime, too. Between planting and harvest, the time when the roadways shimmer from the heat and the sky gives birth to tornadoes. I pass a farmer pitching hay over a corral fence for waiting cattle. Then I'm passed by two Harley Davidson motorcycles, both riders in black leather and bandanas. Shortly afterward, I pass a cow standing in the middle of the road.

Highway 85 is long, narrow, and mostly straight. On the west side, a line of old telephone poles looking like crosses support their wires. News from here to there. Toward the east as well as the west, the world reveals what could easily be endless farmland, grassland, places to roam. As the saying goes, as far as the eye can see. Just west of the road, however, is something the eye can't see—or at least can't see directly. The Burning Coal Vein. Started by lightning, or perhaps a passing grass fire, the vein has been burning for more than a hundred years. No smoke breaks the surface today. It is a slow smoldering. Ten feet burn each year. Sometimes more, sometimes less. When the coal turns to ash, the earth on top collapses and the hills begin to look like stairs. Rocky Mountain Juniper trees are called Columnar Junipers here, their narrow column-like shapes caused by the fumes of the fire.

~

Bugs hit the windshield with the frequency of rain and the sound of gravel. The storm dropping hail in Bismarck has moved over the curve of the earth and I can no longer see it. But there is a haze to the southwest—the kind of haze that surrounds a supercell when seen from the side. I may be driving into weather.

West of the highway are the national grasslands, with a few roads and signs pointing toward access. At the roadside, herds of cattle up against the fence, then flocks of sheep, then fields of hay and grain. A green tractor pulls a red hay baler that turns hayricks out of the back. Twenty minutes south of Belfield and sixteen miles west of a town called New England, on U.S. 85, the Old West Trail, the Can-Am Highway, the land begins to change. Buttes to the east. Ragged hilltops to the west.

This is dry country. Arid. On average, only sixteen inches of water fall here in a year. This is rangeland, where people argue, sometimes hard, about running cattle on federal land.

The sky, however, may bring another harvest. Most of the missiles that used to wait in their silos between the air bases at Grand Forks and Minot are gone. But the hot talk now is about the North Dakota Airspace Initiative. Too much sky with too little beneath it, and so it seems a perfect place for air combat training.

The White Lake National Wildlife Refuge, created by executive order signed by Franklin D. Roosevelt on February 3, 1941, seems to race by the Jeep's windows as the road makes a small turn to the right.

～

On the north side of the town of Amidon, giant round hayricks fill the fields by the thousands. In town, an old police car from the 1940s or 1950s, a white sedan with a single red bubble on top, sits in front of the fire department building and appears to be watching the traffic. The speed limit drops in town, of course, and the cruiser is believable enough to cause some worry. But nobody is behind the wheel. In all probability, nobody's been there for decades. A sign over a store flying a maple leaf flag says, "Canadian Spoken Here."

Amidon fades quickly and the Jeep comes back up to speed. Two miles east and five miles south of the town, though, is the highest point in North Dakota: White Butte, elevation 3,506 feet. White Butte is not a classic flat-top mesa. Seas of mounds, rises, bluffs, and cliffs surround the summit. The earth, where it's cut away from the grass, is white because of the bentonite in the soil and rock. I remember a line from a guidebook I've left back at home, a book describing the high points of each of the fifty states. Regarding White Butte, it says, "Be alert for rattlesnakes in the area. They are very common, and close encounters occur frequently."

There is a part of me that wants to stop here, to go back into Amidon and turn east at the intersection, to find the route that leads to the path to the summit of White Butte. To ask permission at the farmhouse, then to unlock the gate and cross. To say I've stood at the highest point in the state of North Dakota. To believe such an act would count, somehow.

But this is midday, mid-July, in the middle of the country, and I have a long way to go. Motion is the blessing of days like these. Motion, and the illusion that the world is rising over the horizon in front of me and unfolding, revealing itself simply as it is on this one particular day.

~

South of Amidon, another cow has broken through the fence and stands in the middle of the road, its rear end facing me as I approach. A piece of sheet metal has blown up against the barbed-wire fence that defines the highway right-of-way. A wooden billboard with hand-painted letters promises friendly shopping in Bowman and small-town charm. Another sign says, "The Bowman County 4-H Club welcomes you." Then the small green highway sign—this stretch of the highway adopted by the Bowman Future Farmers of America.

Fields of cattle, and then a field of horses.

Even here, a small Federal Express van delivers the world on time.

In Bowman, a sign for the world-famous Big J's Restaurant, the only real food in town. A sign for the Butte View Campground. Lights on a baseball field. A Cenex station and livestock supply, small homes neatly kept, kids rollerblading down a side street. At the Super 8 Motel, the marquee simply reads, "Clean Rooms."

South of town, however, after the Bowman auction sales and a veterinary clinic, the land opens up again. Fields of grass, fields of grain, storm clouds in the southwestern distance. I pass a green John Deere tractor pulling a hay baler and then I'm passed, as if I were backing up, by an old orange Corvette convertible. U.S. 85 is both farm access and drag strip. I push the seek button on my radio. It spins rapidly through the dial, not stopping once—no station is strong enough to capture its attention.

~

Three o'clock and I cross into the state of South Dakota. Still fields of cattle, fields of hay. Buttes and hilltops in the distance. Radio towers stand on a few of them like sentinels, but none broadcast news or music. Telephone, certainly. And perhaps the words of security too. A group of white boxes, beehives, stand in a field on the west side of the highway. Then more of them on the east. These are open lands for grazing. In the west, on a butte, the appearance of evergreens, the beginnings of the Custer National Forest. And then suddenly Tony Blair is on the radio, talking about the moral obligation of liberty. A short distance farther up the dial, a preacher talks about the perfect law.

The town of Buffalo, looking worn, comes and goes. A small bridge crosses the south fork of the Grand River.

A blur in the rearview mirror, and suddenly the orange Corvette passes me again. A man and a woman. The man dark-haired in a white baseball cap, the woman with short blond hair blowing free. Both of them in their late forties or early fifties; they smile and wave as they pass. They could be in a commercial. I saw them earlier, pulled over in a rest area on the south side of Buffalo. The woman had her legs stretched across the seats and was reading. The driver's seat was empty, but there was a line for the men's bathroom. A camper and an RV waited as well.

As they started to pass me this time, an oncoming car appeared over a small rise. I could almost hear the couple say "Oops" as they pulled back in behind me. Then the car passed, the Corvette pulled out and sped by me. All smiles and waves. Summer on a long straight prairie road in South Dakota.

U.S. 85: Mid-July, Midday, Mid-USA

Classic rock and roll on the radio now. Fields of sage both east and west. The storm haze disappears, but the radio says there might be the occasional shower tonight. Clear sky to the west. Fields, rises, hills, small valleys. South of the Badlands, north of the Black Hills, open ground and then the town of Redig. Two trailers and a small convenience store. Not a single home. The radio tells me the temperature is 100 degrees.

A small junction joins U.S. 85 with Route 168 heading east. I have a map, open now on the seat next to me, that says I'm near, if not at, the geographical center of the fifty United States. Mid-USA! The very center of it all! I don't know what I'm expecting, really. Signs. Stores. Souvenir shops. Miniature golf. Some gargantuan fiberglass American flag. One-hour photos. And I don't know what I'm hoping for, either, though I know it's not the silly or the profane. A sundial, maybe. Or just a guest book, a register to sign and say I was here. But so far there is nothing. I slow down, look both ways and ahead and behind. No matter how hard I try, though, no sign, no direction post points me to the spot. Perhaps a little bit farther ahead.

The pavement bends left around a small hill or butte, a blind corner, and before I can hit the brakes I pass a road leading east from the highway, a gate pulled across it, barricaded with a Road Closed sign. A path, a small road runs up to the face of a butte and then perhaps behind it or around to the top. Is this it? Is this the geographical center of the United States of America? Is it possible that at the very center of our country the road is closed?

I'm coasting now. Southbound, away from the center. I have this feeling that I should go back, drive around the barrier, put the Jeep in four wheel-drive, and find wherever that small path leads. I have this feeling that somehow it's wrong, cosmically wrong, to be so close and yet miss the spot. But of course there's nothing real about this spot. The geographical center of North America is several hundred miles north, outside Rugby, North Dakota. To say that this spot, halfway between Redig and Belle Fourche, South Dakota, is the geographical center of the United States is to include Alaska and Hawaii but choose to ignore the whole of Canada. This is the geographical center of a political idea. At best, this spot is only make-believe.

I step on the gas. It's more than 100 degrees outside, yet the first set of permanent snow fences appears. These fences, designed to create dead air and thus trap the snow before it buries this remote roadway and some people along with it, are built with wooden slats, spaced to let some air through, and angled about forty-five degrees from the ground. Rocks begin to appear in the fields—layered, sedimentary. All four directions, not a building to be seen. Fields of sage, dry creek beds, the occasional tree, small buttes. On the radio, the Beatles sing "Sergeant Pepper's Lonely Hearts Club Band," and "I Get By with a Little Help from my Friends."

3:30 in the afternoon, Mid-July, Mid-USA

I crest a small rise on the north side of Belle Fourche and can see the town below and in front of me, houses and signs rising among trees. Beyond the town, however, still only gray in the haze of the midday heat, the outlines of much larger hills—the northern edge of the Black Hills of South Dakota.

Such weight in the distance, the hills exert their own kind of pull, though Belle Fourche gives every impression of prosperity and fun. Although the map places the mark well north of town, signs in Belle Fourche proclaim it's "at the middle of everything!" Near the center of the United States, a small town with a French name that means Beautiful Fork—named before the Louisiana Purchase for the joining of the Belle Fourche and Redwater rivers and Hay Creek.

Small shops, quaint homes, people playing, talking on the sidewalks. A Web site tells me that "Belle Fourche is one of the most important livestock shipping railheads in the West. The wool shipping warehouses are the largest in the US even today." And I learn that "on June 27, 1897, Kid Curry, of the Butch Cassidy–Sundance Kid Hole-in-the-Wall gang botched the robbery of the Butte County Bank (at the site of the present Norwest bank) in one of the funniest episodes documented in the Old West." But the Web site does not tell me the story.

At the gas station, the counters and doorways to coolers are crowded. It's a very hot day and the storm I saw earlier has come together hard and the radio tells me there is wind and hail to the east. In Belle Fourche, however, the sky is clear. Fifty miles to the west—Devils Tower National Monument. Straight ahead of me—the dark shapes of the Black Hills.

~

The whole sight of Spearfish comes and goes. I know there is a canyon here, a beautiful route. Signs promise an authentic mining experience, and a restaurant features crab. U.S. 85 joins the interstate for a few east-bound miles, then leaves it again and heads south into the hills.

This is no longer the western prairie. Now U.S. 85 winds through limestone cutouts and dense forest. A sign tells me I'm entering the Black Hills National Forest—Department of Agriculture. Although it's tough to tell just from looking, my own need to shift and the exhaust billowing from slow-moving semis tells me we're all moving uphill at a pretty good angle. No longer straight, the ribbon of U.S. 85 now twists and turns as it follows the contour of the hills. I pass an area for trucks to check their brakes.

A sign goes by too fast for me to read it well, but in Deadwood I can get either cocktails and a seventy-nine-cent breakfast or cocktails for seventy-nine cents with breakfast. I can gamble; I can eat. Live poker! Hotel rooms available.

Deadwood is all decked out in red, white, and blue banners. It's a place where tourists can gamble at the Holiday Inn. The Super 8 advertises slot machines with the highest payout in town. A motorized trolley car filled with overweight parents and children rolls down the street and passes a hut serving espresso and latte. In the town of Lead, tours are offered of the Homestead Gold Mine.

There is history here. Mining in the Black Hills, mining for gold. To the south and east, Mount Rushmore, Crazy Horse, Sturgis, Wind Cave, Wounded Knee. To the west, Devils Tower and Little Big Horn. And I know that with every mile under the tires, every press of foot on accelerator, I am passing stories I should know better than I do. Any chance to move slowly is a step toward depth and, with any luck, insight. But there are still so many miles for me to travel this day, and history is not the only roadway to understanding a landscape.

A sign with Smokey Bear tells me the fire danger is high today, and south of Lead the forest comes up tight to the roadway, the tall trees sometimes making it difficult to see the sky. The road twists, weaves, turns, sidles, hugs, opens, drops, climbs, bends, shoots, and draws. The posted speeds for turns are twenty-five, then thirty, then twenty-five miles an hour. I have to admit, in the Jeep this is fun.

$\sim$

The highway crosses a small pass—elevation 6,785 feet in the Black Hills of South Dakota—and then U.S. 85 winds its way downward and south toward Wyoming.

Mid-July, early evening now, in the middle of the USA. A sign tells me I'm leaving the Black Hills National Forest. The next sign tells me I'm entering the state of Wyoming. And the sign after that tells me, "Wyoming Is Beef Country."

The earth here is as red as the dirt of South Carolina and Georgia. The pine trees are thick. Forests open up into meadows with wildflowers and small streams. Here and there, herds of cattle cool off in a creek or press up against a fence. Clear sky above. It's a beautiful evening in eastern Wyoming. Although the snow fences give evidence of other seasons, other beauties, and other threats, as does the occasional alert to today's fire hazard, on this wonderful evening it's possible to believe there's more land than there is imagination to fill it. It is possible to believe, just for a moment, that parts of the world remain fresh and undefined by economics or politics.

At the South Creek overlook, looking east from the highway, the view is a wide-open valley in greens and golds. Hills, evergreens, thunderstorms in the distance. Spectacle, I think. Spectacular. Quite a show.

～

On the north side of Newcastle, the road changes to 6 percent downgrade, and U.S. 85 becomes a roller coaster ride down the hill. The views to the west are no longer forest and meadow. Falling out of the Black Hills, the views change to high desert, brown and green fields of sage, hills, buttes in the distance that rise like breakers in front of the Rocky Mountains. When I pass a sign that says, "85 Closed When Flashing. Return to Newcastle," I am reminded that the amber light of a hot summer evening is not the only face this country wears. If this were mid-January, the barrier gate by the sign could be down, the highway could be snow covered, and the wind could raise the snow so fast that the road, and then cars, and then hopes could be buried and then lost much faster than any plow could recover them. These are the things that are possible on U.S. 85.

South of Newcastle, the open country is all grass and sagebrush. In the distance, to the east of the highway, a train pulls two miles, maybe more, of coal cars on a track heading south. Sage grows every place it can. Broad expanses, wide-open spaces, buttes in the distance, theatrical sky—it's a big country in the middle of July.

I pass a wooden sign with *Wyoming* painted in large letters across the top. It's a historical marker for the Robbers' Roost Station.

Robbers' Roost Station. Cheyenne and Black Hills Stage Route. Along the Cheyenne-Deadwood stage route, stories are told of outlaws and buried gold. But the swaying Concord stagecoaches stopped rolling in 1887 eleven years after beginning service to the gold regions of the Black Hills in 1876. Located at the Cheyenne River crossing, Robbers' Roost was a station of the Cheyenne and Black Hills Stage and Express Company. Built in 1877 on a new shortcut, it derived its name from the many robberies in the area. The crossing was the spot most dreaded by stage drivers: steep riverbanks slowed the coaches to a crawl and provided concealment from which lurking road agents could wait the approach of the intended victims.

Station agent at Robbers' Roost was D. Boone May, also a deputy U.S. marshal and a shotgun messenger for gold-laden treasure coaches from the "Hills." In September 1878, south of here, May and John Zimmerman surprised desperadoes in the act of robbing the southbound coach. The outlaws opened fire and one of them, Frank Towle, was fatally wounded. Outnumbered, May and Zimmerman escorted the coach to safety and the outlaws made their escape. Towle was buried by his companions. May later found the grave, removed Towle's head and took it to Cheyenne in a sack to try to claim a reward.

Standing by the sign, a strong wind coming out of the west and the early evening not diminishing the day's heat at all, I can almost imagine the sound and the rock of the stages, and the fear of their drivers and passengers. Large country is often quiet enough to hide in. But then the sign and I are passed by two long-distance bicyclists in spandex shorts and shirts, wearing helmets, all their gear strapped to the frames, biking north on U.S. 85. One of them whistles a song by the Beach Boys.

~

In Lusk, Wyoming, two men sit outside the Conoco station, stretching their legs and resting. In front of them, two motorcycles with license plates from Alaska. On the north side of town, children play and dive in a city pool called the Lusk Plunge. The sun is beginning to set, the high grassland taking on an even more golden glow. Gathering clouds, but not for storms. It's the middle of the evening in the middle of July, in the middle of the country.

At the Conoco station, I ask how far it is from here to Cheyenne in terms of hours. The clerk, a woman in her early thirties, says it's about two. I ask if it would be faster to continue on U.S. 85 or scoot over to the interstate. She says it's about the same. Then a man behind me pipes up. He says, "If you like interstates." I ask him how far it is to Casper, where I've been before. A different man says, "I've made it in 45 minutes." Everybody laughs. If he made it that fast, the clerk says, he must have been flying.

The sign at the bank still says it is 100 degrees, which is no longer true. Spicy chicken tenders from the gas station, six for three dollars, and I'm on my way south. The open ground here has gone from gold to a deepening green. Snow fences, telephone poles, sagebrush, the occasional herd of cattle, a ranch for raising Arabian horses. I'm following a truck for Wal-Mart, even here in the middle of everything.

∼

7:18 mountain time, on U.S. 85 south of Lusk, Wyoming, and I swear I am not making this up. To the east of the highway, two cloudbursts separated by who knows how many miles—ten? twenty?—paint a dark path across the sky as the rain falls in curtains, mists hanging from the clouds. Between them, the brighter sky of indigo and pink. Off to the west, through the clouds, what my children call God light has appeared, shafts of rose-colored light falling from the heavens and illuminating patches of earth. The beams themselves made visible by the mist. There is a smell of sage in the air as the car zips along the highway. Wyoming is performance art, I think. And though I haven't seen a single antelope all day, I'm sure they're out there. I'm sure I see them. This is the middle of July, in the middle of the country, and later, in the middle of this night, I'm sure there will be stars.

The Other Road in Winter

There are places in our lives that simply provoke our curiosity. We hear about them, but not because we asked. We see a picture, but not because we're looking for one. And the story, or the image, stays with us. Something, we're not quite sure what, makes us wonder.

We don't go out of our way to visit these places. We don't say, "I'm going to make a special trip!" But looking at maps for the trips we do take, our eyes begin to wander off course. Something about the name of a town, or the shape of a coastline, or perhaps something as small as the memory of an accent in some grade-school friend's voice, pulls us out of the direct and logical path. We wonder how much extra time it would take to go that way instead of this. We wonder why we're wondering at all. Just to see what it's like, we say. And then we wonder if we can get away with it.

This morning, as the Jeep warms up at a hotel, I am nestled between three lakes: Huron, Michigan, and Superior. Huron I won't see today, the road is already too far inland and the curve of the earth is too steep, though I saw it, and Erie, briefly through rain and snow last night. I am on my way to the Upper Peninsula of Michigan. The road from Baltimore, where I needed to be, and Moorhead, Minnesota, where I live, does not speedily go through any part of Michigan. But I have never seen the Upper Peninsula—"the UP." These roads are close enough. And phrases like "lake effect snow" seem to me more powerful than any siren's song. The temperature is 7 degrees below zero. There is a wind chill advisory, and I'm told there will be new snow this morning. Snow showers at least. Perhaps something more.

Interstate 75 north out of West Branch, Michigan, just north of Saginaw Bay, is remote country. This morning I'm the only car on the road even though it's already 8:30. There is a strong headwind. Snow flurries. The passing lane is glazed and ice covered. Snow drifts down the center of the right lane too. The trees, alternating between deciduous hardwoods and evergreens as the land rises and falls, are stark and forbidding. The sky is overcast with dark clouds. Every now and then a little bit of blue is visible somewhere. The wind whips up what would be dust devils if there were dust. But they're made of snow, tremendous, and they rock the Jeep hard as I go down the highway. I pass a county salt truck and feel like stopping the driver and asking if he'd mind continuing all the way to Minnesota.

Outside the town of Gaylord, I pass a sign that tells me I've crossed the forty-fifth parallel—halfway between the equator and the north pole. Shortly after that, I'm passed by a truck towing two snowmobiles. The Jeep is crusted with white road grime, a good eighth of an inch thick on each headlamp and fender, and the wipers have been working overtime. As I get closer to Mackinaw City, though, the tourist signs appear—everything from the Mackinac Island Butterfly House to rides on a high-speed jet-powered catamaran. Summer fun. And then, as if on cue, as the speed limit drops and the town begins, the overcast breaks and gives way to deep blue sky and cotton-ball clouds.

Coming over a rise, in the distance I can see the two white spires of the Mackinac Bridge, the towers that support the suspension cables, beautiful and gleaming against the sky. The cables fall away toward a roadway I cannot yet see, but the urge to cross is already strong. On the other side is the UP. Above the bridge live UPers. Under the bridge live trolls. On the west side of the highway, two wind generators turn slowly, gracefully in the breeze. This is not a warm morning and the Jeep's heater cannot keep out the cold, so I pull into a hotel's entryway and go inside to warm my feet and change into better boots. The temperature is 6 degrees below zero. As I talk with the desk clerk, we both watch long lines of cars with snowmobile trailers pull into gas stations and then their owners filling the sleds. "So much for a quiet Sunday morning," she says.

A fresh cup of coffee, two hard right turns out of the parking lot, and I begin the climb up the bridge. Five miles from one side to the other. 8,614 feet of suspended bridge. 199 feet above the water at the middle. 42,000 miles of cable. 1,024,500 tons of stuff to get me across, and the simple sight of it is wonderful. "Embracing engineering and beauty," the Web site says.

Once I'm on the bridge, however, it is the lake that knocks the breath out of me. Lake Michigan is frozen. Hard. Complete. A gigantic white arctic scene, complete with pressure ridges and snow boulders thrust up in the distance. All the way west, as far as I can see, ice from shore to shore. And all the way east, around islands and points and rocks, as far as I can see, ice from shore to shore. It's possible to imagine that an icebreaker went through yesterday, or last week, because there is a flat plane of ice much like a road that moves under the bridge and then into the distance, the ice a slightly duller white. But there is no open water this morning. The pressure ridges, rises in the ice where it presses against itself and cracks upward, long and singular, wind like a track left by a snake or by some animal's tail. This is a beautiful, beautiful winter morning.

∼

U.S. 2 heading west from the bridge goes from four lanes to three and then down to two. On each side of the road there are birches, oaks, maples, and evergreens. The highway doesn't hug the shoreline, although frequently they meet each other winding from inlet and cove to point and bluff. Lake Michigan, now to my south and left, remains frozen and unbroken by any clear water. The road itself is dry, grime no longer kicked up by the tires of cars in front of me. At one point the roadway and the lake nearly meet, with no homes along the shore. The pressure ridges look like dunes or hills, and it's easy to imagine wandering off into such a landscape. The call of the expanse is intimate and clear. Wandering off and perhaps never returning.

A sign tells me I'm driving through the Hiawatha National Forest. Once again the roadway and the lake join each other, small sand dunes the only barrier. A sign says, "Watch for Sand on Road." There is a blizzard out there, a ground blizzard. The wind simply picking up the loose snow. I can watch it move across the lake.

To be at lake level—sea level, as it were—against a frozen expanse is very different from looking at it from the bridge. From up there it's scenic. Pretty. Down here at the level of the water, it's humbling and, despite the beauty of this day, just a little bit frightening. I don't know if it says more about me or something about human nature, but as the road heads west, my eyes are drawn to the lake, to the flat and empty expanse. To my right, to the north, there are forests with bears, deer, and other wildlife. But nature abhors a vacuum. So with every turn, every opening in the woods, my attention comes back to the ice, and the snow, and the distance.

⌇

It's not so much that the lake is a vacuum as that it's a part of our imagination not so easily filled. So much surface hiding so much depth. Even a life near water is not enough to diminish the mystery and the allure.

Most of my growing up was done within a mile or two of Lake Michigan, on the North Side of Chicago. I remember going to the beach with my family to play in the sand. We'd be almost brave enough to swim in the cold water. But not quite. One afternoon a log floated by; various cousins and uncles looked at it. We dared each other to go out and touch it and come right back. It was not that far away, we told each other, but the water was that cold. I waded out thigh deep before the cold immobilized me. One of my uncles just splashed and dived in, swam to touch the log, and swam right back. Frozen to my spot, I watched him towel off and sit on the warm summer sand.

I also remember a high school date. Having driven down to the beach to make out in the back seat of my family's car, we somehow lost interest in each other's breath and found ourselves captivated by the rollers coming in. Some storm on the Michigan side of the lake was pushing the waves toward where we huddled. There was a light drizzle that night. Lake Michigan beginning a case of distemper.

I have seen the angry waves as well as evenings when the lake was as beautiful as some Caribbean or South Pacific bay. A thousand days when the lake was just a big bunch of cold water, too. I remember learning about lampreys and how they attach their suckers to fish, and I remember how that made me afraid to swim for a while. I remember a night, somewhere in the middle of college, when two high school friends—Cliff Grost and David Faassen—and I sat on a sailboat in some Chicago harbor and talked the talk of past and future hopes above the reflections of stars and buildings, the world spread out for us on the glassy smooth lake.

Superior, of course, is a different story. I was in my first year of college when the radio stopped everyone cold.

> The legend lives on from the Chippewa on down,
> Of the big lake they called "Gitche Gumee."
> The lake, it is said, never gives up her dead,
> When the skies of November turn gloomy.

I'd never seen Lake Superior, though I'd heard stories from high school classmates who called themselves Voyageurs and spent part of every summer in the Boundary Waters and the Quetico Provincial Park. No one ever spoke about Superior with gentle words. "Does any one know where the love of God goes, / When the waves turn the minutes to hours?"

There are legends about Superior. I don't know if they're true, but I hope they are. I have been told that a drop of water entering the lake at Duluth takes two hundred years to pass under the bridge at Sault Sainte Marie. I have been told that, if you were to spread out the water of Lake Superior a foot deep, it would cover the whole of North America. Every valley, every mountain, every grocery store, every school board meeting.

And I remember an evening in early fall, driving east from my home for a first meeting at a place called Wolf Ridge, an hour north of Duluth. Cresting a hill south of town, I caught my first sight of the lake, green blue in the twilight, smooth enough to reflect the few clouds, spreading south to Wisconsin and the Apostle Islands, spreading east and north to infinity. I pulled the Jeep to the side of the road just to gather it all, and failed.

∼

You cannot mention the Upper Peninsula of Michigan without mentioning snow. David Van Kley, who for many years was a UP pastor before getting a call to the Black Hills of South Dakota, once told me that "the snow will be much deeper in the northern UP, especially inland.

Get off the main roads and you're likely to see incredible snow depths. Everybody who knows the UP and writes about it is always referring to the snow. It is a staple of life, a window to all kinds of truth."

On the seat next to me I have a printout of an e-mail from him, a kind of road map to the stories I will not see.

> At Bessemer, Black River Harbor Road stretches northward about 15 miles to Lake Superior through Ottawa National Forest. At the harbor, there is a breakwall jutting out into Lake Superior. Seagoing boats are docked along the lower reaches of the Black River below Rainbow Falls. Three large waterfalls, including Rainbow Falls, are scattered along the last several miles of the river. Just up the hills from the harbor, Copper Peak Ski Flying Hill is the only ski flying facility in the western hemisphere (ski flying hills are much larger than ski jumping hills).
>
> Side trip—Just east of town, a county road leads about 18 miles north to the mouth of the Presque Isle River on Lake Superior. Here, too, there are many waterfalls, a delightful swinging bridge over the river, and lots of trails along the Lake. This is the western terminus of Porcupine Mountain State Park, about 60,000 acres of hills, virgin timber, and wild lakeshore in the western UP.
>
> Continuing east about 15-20 miles on M-28, you will reach Bergland, where Arlene worked for several years with a CPA. Lake Gogebic, the largest inland lake in the UP, stretches southward from Bergland. It is good walleye water. We did a worship service at one of the campgrounds every summer throughout the summer.

A blue sedan passes me, snow packed a least a foot deep on its roof. It looks like wedding cake.

> Side trip—M-64 goes north from Bergland to White Pine and Silver City. The largest copper mine in the U.S. was located at White Pine, but closed during my years in Wakefield. Just west of Silver City, the highway winds into Porcupine Mtn State Park. A road leads to the Lake of the Clouds overlook, 700 feet above Lake Superior and about 400 feet above Lake of the Clouds, a wilderness lake cradled between the ridges below. This is one of the most often photographed places in the midwest. The road ends here . . . everything else in the "Porkies" is foot traffic only.
>
> East of Bergland, M-28 goes through an area of cleared land, some of

which is used for dairying. The towns of Topaz, Matchwood, Ewen, Bruce Crossing, and Trout Creek lie here. Just east of Ewen, on Cemetery Road (I believe it's the first house on the right, next to the A-frame cottage), my friend and former colleague, Wally Leno, is building his retirement house. If you feel like taking a 5 minute detour and he or Alice are there, you could greet them for me!

Side trip—At Bruce Crossing, U.S. 45 heads north (quite some distance) onto the Keweenaw Peninsula, a rocky peninsula jutting out into the lake. Here are Houghton, Hancock, and Michigan Tech University. At Calumet, is the Calumet National Historical Park, where the first mining craze in America resulted in the settlement of the Keweenaw, followed by labor crisis, violence, etc. The mines here were mostly copper, though small claims of gold and silver also were pursued. North of Calumet, the road enters a beautiful area of forests and hills. The Brockway Mountain Drive soars up to 1,000 feet above Lake Superior, then descends to the shore at Copper Harbor, the tip of the Keweenaw.

Side trip—North on U.S. 41 between L'Anse and Baraga lies Keweenaw Bay. On the ridge overlooking the bay is the huge statue of Bishop Baraga, an early missionary to the Ojibwa in this area, holding a pair of snowshoes. It's called the shrine of the snowshoe priest.

Cars heading the other direction leave plumes of snow from their hoods and roofs. The ice crystals hang in the air, reflecting the now bright sunlight, refracting it too into colors and moods. Very much like a cathedral, I think. Or maybe just a very cool snow globe.

Back on 41/28 near Nestoria, dirt roads lead north into some very wild country, including two large wilderness areas I once spent a lot of time visiting. East of M-95, you enter the Marquette Range area, the most populous part of Upper Michigan. Two large iron mines still form the backbone of range economy. Both the Tilden and Empire mines operate south of Ishpeming and Negaunee. The Empire employs over 2,000 people; the Tilden about half of that. Both are open pit operations . . . though you will see shaft buildings here and there around the range, remnants of the shaft mining era, which ended in the 80's. At Ishpeming is the National Ski Hall of Fame, on the corner of M-28/U.S. 41 and Third Street. Down Third Street about a mile toward town, you would see Bethel Lutheran Church, where I served as a co-pastor for 6½ years. Since my departure, the church caught fire and burned up (not to the ground—it was a brick structure); a new Church stands at the same location and follows the same design. Back on 41/28, the road east of Ishpeming descends a hill alongside Teal Lake into Negaunee. I once lived and went to Church here. The large brick church on the corner of 41/28 and Baldwin Avenue is Immanuel Lutheran Church. I was confirmed as an adult in that place! Emily and Nick were both baptized there.

Continuing east from Negaunee on 41/28, the road becomes a busy 4 lane with lots of development on both sides of the road, leading into the city of Marquette. Marquette is the largest town in Upper Michigan, with a population of about 25,000. I graduated from college here, at Northern Michigan University. Nick has also attended NMU for 2 years. Incidentally, you may see signs here and there for "pasties"—pasties are sort of the UP regional food. They are a simple meat/vegetable pie originally introduced to the area by Cornish miners. I have also seen them for sale up in Lead!

If you take M-28 east from Munising, you'll enter a very lonesome, swampy area known as "the Seney Stretch." For about 60 miles, the land is almost perfectly flat and marshy. Islands of pines break the monotony of the landscape. Locally, this area is known as "pine plain." Just south of Seney on M-77 is the Seney National Wildlife Refuge, home to lots of waterfowl and Sandhill Cranes. There is a nice visitor center and drive through interpretative route a few miles south of Seney.

Continuing on M-28 east of Seney, you cross the Fox and East Branch of the Fox Rivers. These are spectacular brook trout streams, where native fish 5 pounds and up are occasionally taken. Do you know Ernest Hemingway's famous short story, Big Two-Hearted River? The story ostensibly is set along the Big Two Hearted northeast of Seney, but everyone associated with the UP knows Hemingway was writing about the Fox. He was just exercising the fisherman's prerogative of keeping a secret!

There is forest to my right, and when I slow to cross ice on a curve I swear I catch a glimpse of a lone skier moving between the trees.

Side Trip—Up M-123 from Newberry are the very impressive Upper and Lower Falls of the Tahquemenon River. In terms of volume, these falls are second only to Niagara Falls in size in the U.S. east of the Mississippi.

U.S. 2 west of St. Ignace hugs the Lake Michigan shore for about 50 miles. Along here are several picnic areas and campgrounds where you can get out and walk on shores that are alternately sandy or rocky (not granite as with LK Superior shores). I've enjoyed the inland fishing at Brevort and Millecoquins Lakes along here. At Manistique is the jumping off point for several interesting places. The famous Kitchitikipi Big Spring (take M-149 out of Thompson along Indian Lake just west of Manistique—it's not far) is one of the largest natural springs in the country. There's a raft that you can use to pole yourself across the springpond to see the bubbling springs 30 feet below in the pond. There's a lot of big fish in the water . . . browns, I think.

The towns of Sidnaw, Ontonagon, Amasa, Kenton, Watersmeet, and Marenisco are typical UP backwoods towns. You might stop at a bar and poke around. It'll probably be a bit depressing . . . but there is something to be gained there.

The little town of Rock, Michigan in the central UP was a hotbed of communist activism in the 40's. If you poke around, you might learn something about that. The Finns were divided, sort of, into the "Church finns" and the "Red finns."

I like the little locations around Ishpeming/Negaunee . . . mining locations like North Lake, Diorite, etc. Each one has a story. The mining museum east of Negaunee on CR-492 has a lot of information on these places and mine . . . disasters like the Barnes-Hecker, where many people lost their lives.

Woody Guthrie once sang a song about "Calumet in the Copper Country," about labor violence in that area. The National Historical Park in that area, recently established, may be a lode of information about the Copper Country's colorful past. There are also deserted (or nearly deserted) towns and deserted mines all over the place in that area.

My friend, Rudy Kemppainen, could tell you a lot about the UP and also especially about Finnish immigrants in the UP. However, I think he's in AZ for a month or so, now. Should be back by March, though.

A snowmobile crosses the road in front of me. Carefully. Slowly. The driver looks both ways. But after I pass, what seems like dozens cross the road behind me. Barn swallows, I think. The way they dive and dart and loop and shoot in late summer twilight.

Like many backwoods places, the UP has become a dumping ground for state prisoners. There's max prisons in Baraga, Marquette, and Munising.

Seney is still the strange little swamp town it was in the Hemingway stories. A few businesses along the highway and backwoods people all around.

There's a shipwreck museum at Whitefish Point in the NE. The Fitzgerald sank near there. I've never been there, but hear that it's quite the place.

Lots of shipwreck signs along the coast from Munising to Whitefish Bay.

There's still a fair amount of commercial fishing going on around Grand Marais, on the Superior shore, and in the Lake Michigan towns of Naubinway, Epoufette, and St. Ignace.

An isolated lighthouse in Big Bay n. of Marquette is interesting, at the foot of the Huron Mtns. (owned by rich people, established by the Ford family). Big Bay was also the place where the film, Anatomy of a Murder was shot.

Too much, I know, to ever visit, to ever see. History is one thing, and the moment is another. But each line, each hint at a story, makes the landscape larger and the background richer.

~

Driving U.S. 2 west from Epoufette through Engadine and Gould City, it's easy to wonder what it would have been like up here in the early days. There's a lot of snow, and the day is cold and hard. Michigan remains frozen and bright. Before I can get too far, however, the wondering is interrupted by a digital telephone tower and then the roar of engines. The north shoulder of the roadway is marked with a thousand snowmobile trails.

~

At Blaney Park, I turn north on Route 77, away from Lake Michigan, to go see what Superior will look like. To see the north side of the Upper Peninsula. There is snow everywhere, deepening on the roadside with every mile, it seems, and the day is turning cloudy.

At the town of Seney I turn left, west, onto Route 28, after stopping at a BP station. Fifteen to twenty snowmobile riders congregate around the pumps. Those waiting simply idle. Those who have already filled up rev their engines in the afternoon air. All I'm looking for is a cup of coffee to keep the chill away—the Jeep's heater can't keep my feet warm—and, strangely, they don't have it. I start to head west on Route 28, and suddenly the wind comes up, nearly whiteout conditions. Snow blows across the road and the few cars turn on their headlamps. Visibility is poor, yet snowmobiles jet past me on the shoulder. A few miles later the whiteout stops. There is no snow in the air, though the wind is still strong as the sun returns.

For reasons I can't even begin to imagine, I cross one small river frozen solid, and then a mile and a half later I cross another, the water open and flowing. A snowplow clears the south side of the road. Giant plumes arc into the air from its blade.

In the town of Munising, for the first time Lake Superior appears, frozen, flat, ice-covered, to the north. Wind whips loose snow into a fog. A dozen or more ice houses sit on the lake. There are signs for glass-bottom boat shipwreck tours, and an auto accident has occurred on the west end of town. The ambulance arrives just as I do, its lights flashing. The roads are snow covered and slippery, and cars slide through intersections. It's hard, driving the road in winter.

The north shore does not have the dunes and the softness, the gentleness, of the Lake Michigan side. These are rocks and cliffs. Just to the northeast, the Pictured Rocks National Lakeshore. This country's first national lakeshore. Forty miles long, the sandstone cliffs and bluffs were formed more than 440 million years ago, during the Cambrian period and then, much later, the early Ordovician period. What should be in the middle, the sediment falling every day for millions of years, between the layers of rock that remain, is missing. Geologists call this an unconformity. What used to be here, they say, was broken, then eroded, then carried away by tides and wind and rain and ice. Except right here, this rock was covered by debris in the wake of the glaciers.

West of Munising, the roads are snow covered and visibility becomes a problem. Snow-covered sand dunes do appear at the shoreline, however, and then suddenly I'm in a town named Christmas. What I think is a snow squall, a tight band of blowing snow tumbling in the path the roadway makes through the forest, turns out to be the cloud of a county snowplow driving just in front of me.

In Marquette, a city of 20,000 people, a big hospital and a good university, the temperature is 7 degrees below zero, and the buildings nearly steam. The sky is sometimes clear, sometimes obscured by the blowing snow. The streets are slush covered and slick. At the Days Inn, the desk clerk is kind enough to let me walk around the pool several times, the high humidity and the heat warming my legs and toes. A quick stop for gas and I'm on the road again. At the Conoco station, a young girl works the register. As she hands me the slip to sign, a man enters: "Hey, I heard about you at the party last Friday." "Yeah," she says, "I had a bit much." "I heard you were getting pretty wild," he says. "There's nothing else to do," she says to me.

On the west side of Marquette I feel two pulls. The first, of course, is Lake Superior. Solid enough now to hold the weight of a small plane, it glows in the afternoon light. Easy enough, I think, to imagine a hike to the north pole. Easy enough, I think, to imagine any story as possible. And the second pull is the road, U.S. 41, heading away from the lake and toward my home, two states away, where I must be before sleep.

Sadly, but with hope, I turn west. The road soon passes through a cutout, where the path makes a cut in a hill, and the rock on either side is dark gray, almost slate colored, though a much harder rock than slate. The tourist signs are now for iron ore museums, shops, tours, sights. There is snow here everywhere—deep, banked against the roadways, piled in parking lots like abstract sculptures ten or fifteen feet high.

West of Marquette, the roads are a hardpack of ice and snow, sometimes melting, sometimes not. Each corner is its own adventure in stability. There are snowmobiles everywhere. One man races me down the shoulder for miles, jumping driveways, sometimes shifting sides of the road behind me and then flying past. Even though I am only going only forty-five, too scared to go any faster myself, he holds back and paces me for as long as he can before turning and disappearing into the woods.

In Ironwood, just before the Wisconsin border, the marquee at one small hotel reads: "Welcome to Paradise."

From the Notebooks

A single-engine plane slows over the highway. First heading south, it banks hard right and drops several hundred feet until it's heading north and lined up with a runway at the airport in Grand Forks, North Dakota. Beyond the arc of this plane, farther away and slightly higher, twin flying Vs of geese head mostly south. Just south of the airport, a herd of bison graze in a field.

10:30 in the morning and I'm heading west on U.S. 2. West for the whole of North Dakota and then a whole lot of Montana. West toward flatlands, Badlands, and then mountains. Thursday morning on the North American prairie, late September, and the pavement is wet. At 47 degrees, the sky is overcast and gray. Dark bands of clouds string themselves north and south, though lighter sky hints at the spaces. A hard day.

The plane, a dull white against a gray sky, and the geese, a dull brown against the same gray sky. Still, I think. It's still beautiful to see the lines they draw. It's still possible to look at them and think of geometry or ballet.

~

"Cheshire Puss [Alice asked], . . . Would you tell me, please, which way I ought to walk from here?"

"That depends a good deal on where you want to get to," said the Cat.

"I don't much care where," said Alice.

"Then it doesn't matter which way you walk," said the Cat.

LEWIS CARROLL

~

It's been raining for two days. Constant and hard. Severe thunderstorm warnings and watches, cells moving by and dropping a tremendous amount of rain. As I head west this morning, Hurricane Isabel is also heading west through North Carolina, Washington DC, and Delaware, bringing its own drama and its own tremendous rain. Category 5, the strongest possible just a day ago. Weakening, though, as it heads toward shore. I am more than one thousand miles away, but my radio brings me this news. And as the construction ends and my Jeep comes up to normal speed, I find myself dreaming of a hurricane on the Atlantic shore. A storm surge filling basements and lagoons and restaurant kitchens. The wind, a common sight on television, unimaginable in real life, tearing roofs from houses and sending anything large cartwheeling through neighborhoods and plate-glass windows.

I can imagine it all. The gasps and the screams of those who have stayed and those who will return. The tumbled everything. Even though I am nowhere near any of this. Leaps of time and space, I think, are possible, if not already everyday events.

Roadside ditches reflect silver from standing water. The ground can still absorb it, just not as fast as the rain is falling. This has been a summer of drought, a late summer and fall of even harder drought. Brown corn still stands in several fields. Sunflowers, their heads drooping, wait to be harvested. All summer long the farmers waited and prayed for rain. Now their fields are too wet to harvest.

~

August, in Iowa Falls, Iowa, and I find myself pulling up to a McDonald's drive-through window. All I can think about is corn. Corn, over every small hill, in every field. Corn as far as the eye can see and closing the imagination to anything else. Corn.

And in the back of my mind, I hear the words of my friend Paul Gruchow.

> A person born in our time will as an infant be clothed in a diaper made in part of corn and fed a formula based upon corn syrup. That person will grow into adult life sustained in thousands of ways by products made from, packaged in, or manufactured with derivatives of corn, from every kind of food except fresh fish to plastics, textiles, building materials, ma-

chine parts, soaps and cosmetics, even highways. And when that person dies, some laws require that the body should be embalmed—in a fluid made in part from corn.

We have not begun to imagine a life without corn. We have assumed, by default of failing to think about it, that corn is eternal. But is not any more eternal than the buffalo. In fact, because the corn we cultivate shares a common cytoplasm, it would take exactly one persistent pathogen to devastate our culture as we know it.

∽

There are two mistakes one can make along the road to truth . . . not going all the way, and not starting.

BUDDHA

∽

Still at that McDonald's drive-through, I remember that I have a package to mail today. I won't be home early enough tonight to mail it from there. As the woman in the window hands me my coffee and burger and fries, I ask where the post office is. "I don't know," she says. She must see my eyebrows go up—this is not a large town. "Sorry," she says. "I just moved here last week." "Really?" I ask. "From where?" "Hawaii."

∽

The oaks, the elms, and the poplars are all just beginning to turn, shades of yellow appearing in the windbreaks, bits of gold amid leaves otherwise still very green. Even though I'm not so very far away yet, this is not the flatland prairie I know from back at home. In this part of North Dakota, there are hills, valleys, rises, and dips. The roadway climbs then falls, banks left and right, and I smile at the way I can feel my own body move against the Jeep's seat. Press down, lift up, lean sometimes hard if I press my luck around a corner. It is simply fun to drive.

The entrance to the Turtle River State Park in North Dakota goes by, the United States and the Canadian flags flying outside over the entrance, and then a flock of geese, one hundred or more, flying over the highway, heading northeast. The one giant V is both sharp and fluid as the birds move from one position to another. A red-tailed hawk sits on one fencepost. An old whitewall tire sits on another.

~

At speed, warm and dry inside my Jeep, Canadian news coming through the radio speakers, it occurs to me that I have no good reason for being here. I am following no good question, no good purpose. I am not being economical or efficient or even very prudent. This is not the fastest road to get to where I need to be. It would have been easier and perhaps even cheaper to fly from Fargo to Minneapolis, from Minneapolis to Missoula. If I needed to drive, for whatever reason, certainly the interstate is faster, safer, more efficient. But, fast and safe and efficient are not the only goals.

Sometimes we drive, or walk, or camp, or simply get out of town because there is a tear somewhere in our hearts or our minds and we need to find a place, a new place with new stories for healing. Sometimes we light out for the territory only because the old place is the old place and we know it all too damn well. Travel is one of our oldest cures, the process more so than the destination, and so we go when our mind says go.

But there is no disaster in my life right now. No rent or rip or tear that I can point to and say this, *this* is the reason for this trip. So what *am* I doing here? What is the benefit of a road trip like this one?

~

The road to truth is long, and lined the entire way with annoying bastards.

ALEXANDER JABLOKOV

~

I remember a story in *National Geographic* some years ago about the pothole region of North Dakota. I remember looking at the pictures, both from the ground and from the air, thinking this was a part of what I call home that I'd never seen. And I remember making a small promise to myself to be here someday, just to see these things for myself. To be present, even if just for a fleeting moment, at the place itself.

This is a road I've never driven, despite having lived in North Dakota and Minnesota for more than fifteen years. The town of Lakota is just a short distance behind me now. Bright yellow biplanes, crop dusters, parked around a small grass runway there. I've been to a good many grass runways, but never that one. And as the runway dwindles in my rearview mirror, I'm amazed at how the commonplace—the fields, the water, the sky, the birds, the farmsteads and towns and people—can arrange itself into the utterly fresh.

Saving, I think. I am saving this ground, the land between my home and Missoula, via U.S. 2. Not saving in terms of rescue. Saving, in its other meaning. To preserve. To keep. In my case, to make a memory and a story of personal experience. To make a life that is rich in detail.

∿

If you don't know where you're going, any road will take you there.

PROVERB

∿

The sign says, "Broken Pavement Next 14 Miles." Ruts and wheel track depressions, cracks and breaks and simple holes syncopate the slap of rubber on the road, and I find myself drumming on the steering wheel, looking at the texture of the highway the way another person would look at sheet music, trying to read what's coming, offering my own beat to the road song. A funky jazz on a spring morning.

On the north side of the highway, the rail line passes over a culvert, but not a usual one. This is no steel tube placed in the ground and covered with dirt. I can't say how old this culvert is, but the arch could have come from Rome. Stone masonry, with brick facing work. Gorgeous and nearly hidden in the tall grass and reeds. Elk graze in a field on the south side of the highway.

12:45 in the afternoon and I'm nearing Rugby, North Dakota. The geographical center of North America, more or less. The real center, I'm told, is in the middle of a small lake a few miles south of town. U.S. 2 is under construction, new lanes being added, old lanes widened. The speed limit goes down to thirty miles an hour and remains there for nearly twenty miles. In town, the town's water tower is bright orange. A high-visibility fluorescent sign outside the Hub restaurant says, "All Waitresses Are Naturally Sweetened."

My good friend Mary Boyd is from here, I think. I should call her, I think, and get some Rugby stories. Or at least be reminded about the ones she's already told me as our families lingered over dinner. Stories about living next to the prison. Stories about brothers and sisters and the wonderful, dangerous potential of long summer afternoons. But much quicker than I expect, Rugby is behind me and the land again opens to prairies, fields, windbreaks of pine and oak, elm, and maple. The sky still gunmetal blue and gray. There is a mist in the air; wipers on low. The grass is reeds and cattails in the ditches dance in the strong wind.

One o'clock in the afternoon. Tchaikovsky on the radio when I pass the Mouse River, and then a sign for the Denbigh Experimental Forest. Another place I've never heard of, never imagined. Another place to look up, another place to slow down. Another reason to smile.

~

> Thanks to the Interstate Highway System, it is now possible to travel across the country from coast to coast without seeing anything.
>
> CHARLES KURALT

~

I pass a road-killed deer in the middle of the highway. Or, to be more exact, I pass the head of a road-killed deer. Resting upright, eyes open, mouth parted only slightly, as if whispering or inhaling, centered on the white dotted line that separates lanes, only the head remains. The bloody neck gives way to innards stretched out in a diminishing red smear. Where the body is, I have no idea. But the way that deer seems to be looking at the oncoming traffic haunts me for days.

~

> God made the world round so we would never be able to see too far down the road.
>
> ISAK DINESEN

~

A small sign in western North Dakota hangs on a chain-link fence. J4. Behind it, a few tubes and pipes stick out of a graveled square. You could miss a place like this in a cough. You'd never think there was a nuclear bomb right there. You'd never think there was a missile.

The prairie is at one level over this huge, mostly flat, open area. Call it what you want—the heartland, the breadbasket of the country—but the prairie is more than anything else a hope and a fear. The prairie is one large farm. Every year it gives up enough for our country and a large portion of the world. We have a history of abundance and trade and occasionally even generosity.

But we have this other history, too. A preparation for war. Solid offense as solid defense. These silos, and the air bases nearby, are here because here is so very far away from the things we are afraid of. It would take a long time for an enemy's missile to reach North Dakota. Long enough for us to react.

I watch as a military helicopter, five hundred feet above the ground, follows the highway back east. A sign tells me silos J1 through J5 are off to the right.

I can't tell you if it's true, but the common story is that in the old days, North Dakota was the third largest nuclear force in the world. Only the rest of the combined United States and the Soviet Union were more lethal. And with the B-52s in Minot, the tankers in Grand Forks, and the fighters in Fargo, the North Dakota air force was the world's best and most dangerous.

But after J4 I am passing grazing cattle and endless prairie. The sunlight is diffused by high clouds and the world looks soft. Pretty. So much going on, I think. It's easy not to see the resources here. It's easy not to see both the metal and the wheat, and even easier not to think about the flesh of the men and women who work on both sides of J4.

2:40 in the afternoon. 1:40 mountain time. 3:40 in Washington DC. 8:40 p.m. in London; 11:40 in Moscow; 4:00 tomorrow morning in Beijing.

〜

Our country is now taking so steady a course as to show by what road it will pass to destruction, to wit: by consolidation of power first, and then corruption, its necessary consequence.

THOMAS JEFFERSON

〜

A short while later, the first sagebrush shows up along the roadside. I know I'm in the west. When I finally reach the town of Ross, the sky has changed—bright blue with white cotton ball, puffy clouds. Farm ponds now reflect deep blue instead of gunmetal gray. The fields that were golden before are almost an electric amber now. The sunshine on the prairie—the western prairie of North Dakota—is bright and hopeful. On the west side of town, hay is stacked to look like humans—a body, two arms, two legs, and then painted smiles and eyes—one male, one female—like Raggedy Ann and Andy.

This is huge country. When the road crests a small rise and you can see for miles in the distance, your heart swells. "This is my prayer," Sade sings on the radio. And I suddenly have a thought—What if we have it backward? What if salvation is not by faith but by works? So many religions, so many rules, so many faces of God in text and in history. What if faith doesn't mean anything at all? What if it's only by works, only by the way we've behave, that we're able to get into the Kingdom of Heaven? What could we say about the prairie and the work that is going on here? Could we say this is a holy place?

On the radio I learn that Hurricane Isabel has moved ashore; nearly a million people are without power. Residents have moved into schools and hotels and shelters. The wind is blowing more than a hundred miles an hour. And I learn that more soldiers have been killed in Iraq. It all seems a very long way away. The sun shines on the brown fields west of Williston, North Dakota, as U.S. 2 straight-lines into Montana.

∼

Central Iowa, middle of August. The temperature is 102 degrees Fahrenheit and the pavement melts into my boots whenever I step out of the Jeep. Hotter than hell is the easy cliché. But then on the radio: "We are moving ahead with our plans to mail the Jesus video to every household in Iowa. Every home deserves the right to see this wonderful Jesus video. But first we need to make sure our prayer base is strong. A strong prayer base is essential for a project like this. We begin with prayer. And this could take some time."

Yes, I think. This could take some time.

∼

I have noticed even people who claim everything is predestined, and that we can do nothing to change it, look before they cross the road.

STEPHEN HAWKING

∼

A roadside historical marker tells me this is buffalo country and describes how the plains tribes used the buffalo. I look around, then climb a fence for a better view. Not one buffalo anywhere in all four directions.

West of Glasgow, Montana, I smile as a pheasant crosses the road in front of me, walking like an overgrown partridge, unaware of the Jeep coming at it faster than a mile a minute. Less than half a mile farther on, though, I have to slam on the brakes as I round a small bend and ten, maybe twelve of them are standing in the middle of the road looking away from me. They scatter and I drive on.

The radio station out of Glasgow, the only station strong enough to be picked up here, gives me the complete high school and college football roundup, mentioning players by name and anecdotal history, as if the entire state knows these young men well enough to call them by their first names.

A train pulls up to the left side of the road, a mile and a half, maybe two miles long. Boxcars heading west. To the south, the cliffs and buttes of the Missouri breaks; to the east, just rolling prairie and farmland, stripes of gold, wheat stubble, stripes of black dirt where the stubble has been turned.

Ahead of me, the hard light of the setting sun but still no sign of the rising mountains, though I know they're there. How soon before the flatland leaps into the Rocky Mountains?

The radio station plays a song by Madonna, and I find myself wondering what it must be like to be an eleven-, twelve-, or thirteen-year-old in a town like Glasgow, listening to Madonna, listening to stars from so very far away. I wonder if you can grow up in a place like this and not want desperately to get out, and not realize until you're gone what a bit of grace it was to be born here. This is not a romantic vision. There is poverty here and hardship and bad weather and a summer without rest. But there is grace here too. The visual grace of fields stacked with round or rectangular hay bales. The mountains between here and the easy distance, the simple beauty and arc of the sky that goes across the day. These things are not attractive to children, but they should be.

I pass a sign telling me I'll find dinosaurs at the county museum.

∾

Interstate 29 in hard winter. Heading north, heading for home, we pass a billboard for Yankton, South Dakota. An invitation to visit, to be a tourist. On the billboard, Lewis and Clark and Sakakawea stand as trio, the trinity of the northern prairie. Sakakawea points meaningfully westward. Such a shame, I think, that she was never here.

~

What you've done becomes the judge of what you're going to do—especially in other people's minds. When you're traveling, you are what you are right there and then. People don't have your past to hold against you. No yesterdays on the road.

WILLIAM LEAST HEAT MOON

~

A hot August night in Alexandria, Minnesota, and I pull in off the interstate to get gas, coffee, candy to keep me awake for the last two hours home.

A young woman, employee of the station, college age, gathers trash from the plastic barrels between the pumps and struggles with their weight. She looks at me and says, "Wish I had your job instead of this one!"

Good humor and smiles. So a minute later I tell her I'm taking up a new profession. "What's that?" she asks. "Butterfly collector," I say, pointing to the grille of my jeep.

Thousands of yellow and red splotches cover my windshield and fenders. But on the radiator, butterflies, wings spread, look as pretty as museum mounts. Monarchs. Yellow moths, a dozen others I don't know. The woman looks at the collection. "Eeewww," she says. Then she moves closer. "This one's really pretty."

~

O public road, I say back I am not afraid to leave you, yet I love you, you express me better than I can express myself.

WALT WHITMAN

~

On the radio, the president of a Montana chamber of commerce talks about the holiday weekend, kicked off by a big-beard contest. There are prizes for the longest, the scruffiest, the best salt-and-pepper. Then there will be a reenactment of a famous trial from the district. It should be an exciting weekend, he says. There's a parade as well, and the Canadian Friendship Barbeque.

With Hurricane Isabel, the radio says, two million people without power; three dead. Surprisingly little damage to property. The weather people say the most dangerous day is not the one when the hurricane hits shore but the day after, when everybody thinks it's safe and the inland flooding begins.

I pass a small white cross on top a metal stake, a marker where somebody has left the road and died. There are an awful lot of them along U.S. 2, most of them multiples—two crosses, three, sometimes four, many decorated with flowers. Some of the crosses are rusted, many are weather-worn, having seen summer heat and blizzards.

It's a warm night at the end of summer on the American prairie. Geese have settled in the fields, ducks have settled on the ponds. I race trains—beating them only barely at my 75 miles an hour.

What May Be Coming

Sometimes you get an idea, and it just won't go away. It lingers in the back of your mind or the front of your memory. It pops up at odd times, a desire completely unexpected. Someday, you think, you'd like to do something extraordinary. You spin a globe and let your finger rest lightly over its whirl. I'll go wherever it stops, you think. Mongolia. Burkina Faso. Santa Fe. Or you spread your fingers over a map to connect the edges. How far, you wonder, from edge to edge? How many stories, you wonder, in between? You smile at the thought of the adventure, and then turn to something else. But sometimes you get an idea, and it just won't go away.

Day One

Ten minutes before eight o'clock on a Thursday morning in July, and I'm standing close to the southernmost point in the whole United States, on a beach in Key West, Florida. The beach isn't natural. A seawall holds the sand against the higher ground. Every so far, steps are cut in the seawall for people who want to move from sand to swell, but the ocean side of this beach has a rocky bottom, what looks like stone and coral and muck. It's low tide, and this is no place for frolicking in the surf.

Even so, I'm standing knee deep in the water with—in my mind at least—one leg in the Gulf of Mexico, one leg in the Caribbean, watching birds flying a bit offshore, tugs and barges and cargo boats in the distance. The only other person I can see is the man who drives the large green city tractor that lifts the sand, strains out the garbage, replaces it smooth and bright for the tourists who'll come here after breakfast.

Already this morning, in town, I've seen men and women working the streets with leaf blowers and brooms, joggers in every color of spandex or cotton, bicyclists, families with wide-eyed children out beginning their tour, the countless chickens strutting through intersections.

Leaving the hotel this morning, I'll admit I did not ask for directions. This is not a large island. Dead reckoning to find the southernmost point led me to dead ends. One took me to the gates of Fort Andrew Jackson. Another took me to a side entrance. Yet another led me to the dock for a cruise ship. Seagulls. Finally, though, on the outside bend of a small side street, there it was. Fat, striped, vaguely buoy shaped, the marker for the southernmost point in the United States of America. I got out of the Jeep, walked around the marker, touched it, took a picture. It's wrong, of course. There are a few hundred yards of more southern land, but none of it open to civilians. Still, this is close enough. Beyond the marker, small waves and giant sky. Seventy miles west, the Dry Tortugas. Ninety miles south, Cuba.

To the south and the west, the sky is blue. Cotton-ball clouds—the promise of a beautiful day in the Keys. To the north and the east, a receding thunderhead—brilliant over the ocean. This is a picture for somebody's textbook. There's a pelican now, slow motion, skimming the waves.

It's a beautiful morning in Key West. Locals and tourists greet each other on the sidewalks. The weather is mild and not too humid. Yet, I must confess, the one thing I want most this morning is to leave, is to fire up the engine in the Jeep, point the car east and then north, and get out of here. That's the whole reason I am here. I am here to begin, to leave, to hoist anchor and unfurl the sails, to finish the countdown and get this rocket going. I am where the road begins—mile zero, Highway 1, just shy of the southernmost part of the United States—and my goal is to drive to the north shore of Alaska, to Prudhoe Bay at the end of the Dalton Highway, to where the road for the United States, at least, is no longer possible.

I've been in Key West before. Thirty, maybe thirty-five years ago. So long ago that I don't remember anything more than cats at the Hemingway house and a very good dinner with my family. And I've been most of the places between here and there, although I've never been to Alaska. But having been someplace before, or not, isn't the point of this trip. This isn't a trip to see something new. This is a trip to see something together—to see what sense can be made of a place where we live by seeing it all at once.

I remember, for example, Florida, Disney World, when I was thirteen or fourteen and never since—long before Epcot. I remember visiting relatives living in Florida, fishing on the Intracoastal Waterway. I remember driving through Georgia, Alabama, Kentucky. All these events, though, separated by years, sometimes many years, and fluid histories. But I've never done it as one trip. I tell people I live in North America. But, I don't really know what North America looks like, except for scattered memories so far apart that it's barely the same person looking at them.

What sense can be made of a country, a continent, by putting it all together in one high-speed road trip? I'm not stopping this time. I'm not stopping to visit people in small towns to figure out who they are or what their lives find urgent. In a way, that's none of my business. People all over the planet have private lives and, finally, I have no interest in using the outsider's lens to expose them. But the trip between this southern beach and the northern one I imagine is as much a trip through history as it is through geography or memoir, a trip through people and places both past and present. There are mountains between here and there, and the remains of mountainous events.

There are people at every turn. And one thing that makes me smile this morning is knowing there are people in this near future who lead public lives, social lives, lives that are geared toward welcome and grace. The minute I turn on the ignition in my car, a whole community opens up to me. Every desk clerk in a hotel, every restaurant server, every gas station attendant will know today and tomorrow and the next day exactly who I am. I am a traveler between one faraway place and another, in need of something they offer. Fuel, a meal, a place to sleep, a story. And I will know exactly who they are—people who for centuries have provided welcome, solace, and comfort for those who are not at home. There is this thing, I've learned, called the law of oriental hospitality. This law, or better yet, tradition, is what caused Lot to offer his own daughters. And the tradition will protect me, too. Wouldn't it be interesting if the earliest expression of the verb "to hope," in any language, was the knock on a stranger's door, the traveler meeting the host? These people will not be strangers to me no matter where I am, no matter whether I've ever seen them before or will ever see them again.

On the beach in Key West this morning, as I look to my right, satellite dishes point toward outer space, radio towers bring and send the news. As I look to my left, people fish from a long pier and a thunderstorm both builds and recedes. Fishing boats head out for a day's work on the reefs, taking happy tourists trying to land the one big fish to hang on the wall. I dip my hand in the Atlantic Ocean. Warm, the smell of fish. I sprinkle some water on my face. It's time for this trip to begin. Somewhere, many miles in front of me, is another ocean, the Arctic Ocean. I want to taste that too. I want to taste that ocean and every mile in between, every flat, every mountain, every valley, and to do it as pretty much the same person. I want to say I've seen the place where I live.

∽

8:10 in the morning and I cross a channel that takes me over to Shark Island. By the Key West AIDS Memorial a sign reads, "Yoga by the Sea—It Sets You Free." Joggers, far too pale to be local, run on the roadside with weights and big arm motions. Another sign tells me, "U.S. 1 in Florida Keys, Eight Fatalities This Year. Drive Carefully." Behind me now, at the Key West High School, there was a sign that said, "2004 Grade A: Job Well Done."

The thunderclouds loom larger and darker in front of me. The traffic on U.S. 1 is not heavy, though there is a good bit of it. We all speed along at forty-five to fifty miles an hour.

To my right this morning, the Atlantic Ocean is calm, a slight wind chop on top of the water, the tiny ripples that sailors hope for on lakes. To my left, the Gulf of Mexico is likewise smooth and just rippled where the wind kisses the surface. From the bridge crossing Shark Channel, I can see beyond the hedgerows and houses to see how flat the Keys really are. Two- or three-foot rise in the tide, it seems, much more modest than the six-to-ten-foot rise that would come with a hurricane, and this would all be underwater. But this is a popular place. A man and his son launch a boat from a boat ramp while another boat motors out toward the thunderstorm. Cars heading west pull boats to launch sometime later.

So here's a question: What is the attraction of the Florida Keys? It's warm, yes. But no warmer than anyplace at this latitude. Texas or Baja California would do just as well. It's marine. But there is a lot of other coastline to prefer, if you wish. The landscape here is not thrilling. It is flat and brush covered. The soil is not good. So why do people seek out this place?

When Ponce de León sailed by and did not stop in 1513, his sailors gave Key West the cheery name of Los Martires, the Martyrs. Some years later, legend described how the first European explorers on the island found the beaches covered with the bones of the Calusas, who had been driven into the Keys by stronger tribes, themselves forced south by the European advances, and named the place Cayo Hueso, Bone Cay. Key West, or more exactly Fort Zachary Taylor, was a Union outpost during the Civil War, and the blockade of southern ports was partially enforced from the harbor there. The battleship *Maine* had sailed from Key West when it blew up in Havana, and the ship's dead are buried here. Comically, this is also the heart of the Conch Republic, the nearly perfect idea just a few years ago. A group of islands decided to secede from the United States, immediately declare war, then immediately surrender, then immediately apply for massive foreign aid.

What brings people here, of course, is the fact that this is a border, an edge, a limit, an extreme. Wherever two systems meet, the world gets just a little bit funky. The drama is underwater—the coral reefs, the wildlife, the fishing. From the Jeep, I believe every third shop on U.S. 1 is a dive shop. And from the Jeep I believe there are a hundred times a hundred fishing boats for charter to chase swordfish and marlin and bonefish and grouper. Part of the attraction is simply to be where those things are happening, to be close to drama.

In the Keys, you get that sense of extremity, of saying, I've been at the beginning or the end, of saying I've gone as far as it's possible to go. And then, willingly, just a little bit farther.

On my weather radio, NOAA—the National Oceanic and Atmospheric Administration—gives the weather forecast for sixty nautical miles out. Seas today, one to two feet. Near shore, smooth water. As I cross the channel to Cudjoe Key, I see half a dozen men and women standing on the old bridge fishing, hoping, even this early in the morning, for something to strike. Most of the bridges here do not allow fishing, but occasionally there's an old bridge or some other structure that you can angle from.

The road turns wet where the thunderstorm has only recently passed. The couple in front of me in a convertible are apparently still dry. Behind me, though, back toward the west, a startlingly brilliant rainbow appears. Lower, a flatter arc than I've seen before, but a beautiful sight in the rearview mirror. There is no intent to a rainbow, no meaning or metaphor—refraction does not mean anything, except of course what we make it mean. But no matter how old we get and how many times we've seen rainbows, it's still surprising and beautiful when they happen.

Now, I think, I am under way.

~

Crossing the bridge over Kempt Channel, leaving Summerland Key, I'm struck by the many different shades of the water. Green, yes. And blue. But also aquamarine, sapphire, electric pink, neon yellow. There's a brown in there, and a black, and a red, though my adjectives fail to give them anything like the power they have. I do know that, in truth, the water here is itself mostly just clear and what I'm seeing is some combination of sky, coral, reflected shore, channel depth. But it doesn't matter. To talk about Matisse only in terms of brushstrokes, or Bach in terms of thirty-second notes, is to miss the point entirely. The fact remains, as I still follow the convertible—top down, North Carolina license plates reading "First in Flight"—that we're moving through a painted landscape.

The storm moving out to sea here was either a doozy or drainage is very bad. The street sides are covered in water. On the concrete footing for a utility tower just offshore, black cormorants hold their wings out to dry.

"Drive with caution; you are entering an endangered species area. Speed kills Key deer." Crossing over onto Big Pine Key, these signs, black letters on highway yellow, tell me I'm approaching the habitat for the key deer, a miniature deer found only here. Their ancestors were normal deer, but when the ice age ended and the glaciers melted, the waters rose and suddenly there was nowhere else to go. Over time, the species got small on the island. They share the key with Mobil stations and trailer courts, appliance stores, mortgage companies, restaurants, coffee shops.

The sign says, "Endangered Key Deer Next Three Miles." Beyond that sign, a florist shop. On the north end of the key, black chain-link fencing suddenly defines the edge of the highway and separates the landscape from the traffic—designed, I would imagine, to keep the deer and automobiles from meeting. A small round blue highway sign shows the symbol for a hurricane and says, "Evacuation Route." What do key deer do in a hurricane, I wonder.

Big Pine is the dividing line between the Lower Keys, starting with Key West, and then the Middle and Upper Keys. There is a change in the limestone and a change in the state of mind. South of Big Pine, people say they live in Paradise. North of Big Pine, they do not.

As I cross the Bahia Honda Channel, I see sailboats at anchor, people moving about them in the morning, getting ready to come ashore or head out to sea, and I find myself wondering what that kind of life must be like. Eight hundred islands, more or less, make up the Keys. Mangrove and sea grass and coral and limestone. Manatees and pirate history. And one long road. Forty-two bridges make U.S. 1 a spine in the islands.

8:52 in the morning. I cross a bridge leading to Ohio Key and can't stop looking at the sign. Ohio Key? How in the world did there get to be a key called Ohio? Later tonight I will look this up and learn that Ohio Key is privately owned, that the place was once Little Duck Key, but men from Ohio building the Flagler railroad renamed the place. I'll learn that this Little Duck Key is not the current Little Duck Key, and that the current Little Duck Key used to be called Big Money Key and Pacet Key. Most keys, I learn, have changed names a good many times. I cross onto Missouri Key and wonder again. Tonight I'll learn that those same railroad guys renamed this place too. It used to be Little Grassy Key. And I'll learn about the railroad. Henry Flagler began the project in 1906. Every bit of it brought in from the outside and running through swamp as well as over open water, the project was finished in 1912, with Flagler riding north from Key West in a private car, only seventeen months before his death. Then in 1935 the second strongest hurricane in recorded history would blow the whole thing into the sea.

～

I'd always thought the Florida Keys were pretty much a straight line of islands, the tops of one sweeping barrier reef connected by the roadway.

I'd imagined that, of course, because of the roadway itself. This morning, though, on the Gulf side of U.S. 1 from Missouri Key, and then Little Duck Key, I notice a number of islands in the distance. Two miles, maybe less. And I wonder what they are; who is there? I wonder what it would be like, seriously, to live even for a short while on an island with nothing and no one else. A cliché, I know. A stereotypic and dangerous bit of selfish romance. But I bet it would be good, too. Good to get disconnected. Good to feel one's own heart at night instead of the press of some morning meeting.

A sandy beach on the Atlantic side of Little Duck Key and I see an old woman wading out into the calm ocean with a pair of lime-green flippers, children sitting in plastic kayaks.

9:01 in the morning and I am crossing Seven Mile Bridge. On the Atlantic side, a small boat at anchor flies a dive flag. On the Gulf side, a ketch sails by—large white canvas filled with just a gentle breeze. It's a beautiful morning in the Florida Keys. Just last night, driving down here, the world was very different. An orange crescent moon setting about eleven o'clock in an overcast sky. No stars. Smooth ocean. No way to tell where water ended and sky began. Quiet, too. How frightening it must have been to sailors before GPS and radio. Even last night, how narrow the drive was, the headlight beams the end of the imagined world.

On Pigeon Key and Key Vaca, there are palm trees. Storefronts here fly the American flag and then the Cuban. The thunderstorm has moved out to sea or fallen apart. A sign for a hurricane shelter points to a utility office.

On the radio I get the Reef Report, dive captains calling the radio station from their boats. They call in height of the seas, strength of the currents, strength of the winds, and visibility. Visibility underwater this morning, I learn, is fifty to seventy feet. A beautiful day for diving. One of the captains calls in from the underwater Christ of the Deep statue off Key Largo. At the end of the Reef Report the dive shop that sponsors it says they have a part-time opening for a captain. They're looking for more trips, more people.

Tourists on the Long Key fishing bridge take pictures of each other fishing. Men, pale skin, shirtless. Women with equally pale skin in tank tops and shorts, baseball caps. Every one of them with a huge grin.

9:52 in the morning and I pass the hurricane monument on Mate-cumbe Key. The real number is vague, but close to 190 victims of the 1935 hurricane are cremated and resting here—423 is the usual number for total storm dead. And that was just one storm. Today the ocean is just a warm and bright playground. So many storms since then—Andrew, Floyd, Camille, Ivan—and so many days of bliss.

I pass through Islamorada and suddenly I'm on Key Largo. No bridge, no causeway brings me here—or maybe I simply wasn't paying attention—but even though there are signs to remind me that this is a hurricane evacuation route, this route could be anywhere. Dive shops, restaurants, hotels, marinas, gas stations, banks, realtors all frame the roadway. You can't see the ocean from U.S. 1. The license plate on the car in front of me reads "MyFlorida.Com" and rests in a frame for the Boston Red Sox.

As I cross the Tarpon Basin Drive, emergency crews, the fire department, and police are all over the middle of the road on the west side of the highway. It's tough to tell what's happened, except that a motorcycle hangs from a tow truck. There are at least seven police cars, two or three fire trucks, a wrecker, and the assorted motorists who've stopped to get out, point, and talk. One policeman walks the pavement with that little wheel that measures distance.

Key Largo is a place I've been before. I remember flying in on a small airplane, swimming in a lagoon, watching dolphins, going deep-sea fishing. My cousin still comes here occasionally. But I haven't been here recently enough to recognize a thing from the road. So many miles still to go today. I look for anything familiar, then press on the gas. I pass a sign that says, "Crocodile Crossing Next Eight Miles." And it doesn't strike me for several minutes that this is strange. I didn't think there were crocodiles in Florida. I thought they were alligators.

~

When you travel, you pack your bags with the stuff you think you're going to need—the shirts, the pants, the underwear, the socks, the toothbrush, the comb. You try to pack as light as possible because it's difficult to carry all that stuff around. When you travel, you also carry another kind of baggage. It's your memories—things you've heard, things you've seen, things you've half-heard and half-seen. In the Upper Keys and then crossing onto the mainland, I find myself thinking about an afternoon in the suburbs of Chicago when I was eleven, maybe twelve years old, attending summer day camp. The campers were divided into Indian tribes. My group of boys, all five or six of us, were called the Seminoles. The Seminoles, of course, are a Florida Native American tribe, the "people who never surrendered." But they are a long way from indigenous. No mention of them is made by any early explorer, though Apalachees, Timucans, Tocobagas, Calusas, Tequestas, and Matecumbes all find their way into diaries. Sometime in the 1700s, Native Americans from the north moved into Florida in huge numbers—most likely to avoid the Europeans. The word Seminole itself could mean wildness or even runaway. Perhaps a combination of peoples running out of both time and territory, the idea could have been "last hope."

I don't remember much about that day in camp except that we had to be silent for about two hours during our initiation, sitting under a tree. Then the older boys made us lie on a bed of twigs, which was supposed to be painful but wasn't, while they smashed berries all over our chests. Then we ran around and hollered like chiefs. I remember reading a book about the Seminoles that afternoon, or maybe it was the week before. I read about how Chief Osceola was captured under a flag of truce and taken to a prison in South Carolina. The book said he died there of a broken heart. That seemed awfully romantic to me at age eleven or twelve, to die of a broken heart, pining for your lost people. I wish I could find that story again, because I no longer think it was a broken heart that killed him.

What history there is in a place like this! Bones on the beaches of the Martyrs. Invasion by the Spanish from the east in search of gold. Invasion by the Spanish from the west and north as well, if I remember my history right, as they came over the arc of the Gulf of Mexico shore in search of the Fountain of Youth. Invasion by other tribes. Incursions by pirates. Then the onslaught of money, real estate developers, tourist shops and seashell sellers, T-shirt factories. And every summer, the lethal weather rising out of the surf.

On the north side of Key Largo, the roadside hedgerows seem trimmed by some machine, vertical, then back at a forty-five-degree angle. Gone wild at the top in this part of July, the hedges nonetheless give the impression of being maintained or manicured. The ocean and the Gulf, on my right and left, are barely visible through the long, manicured hedgesrows. Neither more than twenty yards away. Both nearly invisible.

~

11:04 in the morning and I get off U.S. 1 to begin the Florida Turnpike. All five forward gears, and I'm cruising at seventy miles an hour—a rush after the stop-and-go of the Keys. Coming up to speed makes me smile, makes me feel that something is being accomplished, that this is what's supposed to be. Much the same way as a sail filling with wind or your back pressed against the seat when an airplane bursts down the runway, coming up to speed on a highway is a destination or goal all in itself.

This is still a hurricane evacuation route, but the ocean is too far away for me to see it from overpasses anymore. Palm trees dot the median and the side of the highway. The sky is still clear and blue. Cotton-ball clouds; no storms I can see. Signs point to the Everglades National Park. New townhomes and condominiums with terra-cotta roofs seem in process the length of both sides of the road. Homestead, Florida. License plates from Nevada, Mississippi, Wisconsin. A sign for the Monkey Jungle is followed by a sign for the Southgate Governmental Center.

Seventy-five miles an hour on the Florida Turnpike. I'm thinking about my friends who are pilots, who go flying just to be up there, just to log some hours. Simply to see, to get a different view of the landscape, to be in motion, to be able to turn and have the world rise to greet you. Likewise, my friends who are sailors put out in the morning, not to get someplace, but to feel the press of the wind transferred to the whole of the boat and then made into motion. On the road, the feeling is the same. Every sixty seconds or less, another mile under the wheels. And every mile bringing with it a new way of looking at the world. In southern Florida I cross canals and waterways. I drive by creeks, boatyards, auto stores, cattle farms—all of it unexpected. The ugliness as well as the beauty—all of it fresh.

11:30 in the morning and I pass the exit to Miami International Airport. A large jet, on final approach, crosses the turnpike. A gravel pit on the left side of the highway, and then a lake.

There are people on this road who like to have fun. There are those that don't. I've passed three tollbooths so far. At the first one I drove up, rolled down my window, and said, "Hello." The woman inside answered, "Hello, how're you doing?" We had one of those conversations—a sum total of twenty seconds—that was simply fun and pleasant. A way to greet each other. At the second toll plaza I told the collector I needed a receipt, or two or three. She smiled. She said she had about twenty already made up. I said, "Well, I'll take 'em all!" But she gave me only one. At the third booth, the woman was more dour. "Hello," I said. "Hello." "I need a receipt," I said. She said nothing and looked away as she handed me the white sheet of paper. I still had the car in neutral when I pressed on the accelerator. She heard the engine roar. Then I smiled at her. She did laugh, finally. I said, "I also need to put it in first gear." She said, "Have a good trip."

Earlier, at a bank today, I stopped in to get some cash. The teller asked me how much I needed. I told her $35,000. She looked at me, nearly petrified. Then the teller behind her, and the teller at the next window, both smiled and laughed. Checking into the hotel last night, after I got to the room, I had to walk back to the front desk because the phone hadn't been turned on. The clerk looked at me standing in the lobby, smiled, and said, "I don't even want to know." Getting into the room had been an adventure in itself, since my reservation had been bumped from another hotel and the hotel I was bumped to then sold my room to someone else. I looked at her and said, "You know, in the bathroom, in the toilet, there is this rat. It's about two feet long." She got this look on her face, horrified, surprised, apologetic all at once, and then I smiled. She hit me on the shoulder and said, "Oh, just stop it!"

I don't know any of these people. I have never seen them before and probably will never see them again. Yet on the road we're friends. We understand one thing about each other's days—the act of travel—and on that understanding we can build a day twenty seconds at a time. Coming up on the Red Road exit on the northwest side of Miami, listening to a smooth jazz station, I pass a little red Miata. A man driving, a woman in the passenger seat, his finger on the steering wheel taps, her hand on the rolled-down windowsill also taps. I see they're in time with the music I'm listening to in the Jeep. She glances over my way on the downbeat, and I nod in time. She smiles, turns to her partner and tells him. He turns, looks at me. On the next downbeat, I nod and they tap. We all smile. The traffic opens for them. They hit the gas and are gone. I'll never see them again. But that one small thing can make something pleasant, in this case a memory. That one small thing can often also do more.

The exits for Fort Lauderdale come and go, and a sign tells me I'm leaving the Seminole Indian Reservation.

～

White egrets by the dozen stand in the canals and roadside waterways. In the past few minutes I've passed saw grass, live oaks with Spanish moss, sugarcane, a license plate from Pennsylvania, long-leaf pines. I've passed a sign telling me the next thirty-seven miles are a Wildlife Alert Area. And I've passed what seems like a dozen memorials, round signs reading Drive Safely that show where someone died. Many of them are decorated with flowers. One had flowers and a three-foot teddy bear. Several of them simply rust.

Not so very far from here—just a bit behind me now and west, in the everglades, though I'm not sure exactly where, is the spot where ValuJet flight 592 ended after an oxygen generator, improperly carried as cargo, caught fire. Another memorial there, too.

So many stories, so many histories, so many different ways of explaining where we are.

To the west of me, in the near distance, citrus groves of some sort. Row after row of squat trees, the pathways between them momentarily visible as the Jeep speeds by. To my right, high-tension power lines. The palm trees in the median are well manicured; the grass on both right of ways and in the middle is freshly cut. Everything is well ordered—the crops, the power lines, the roadway, the height of the grass.

As I enter Okeechobee County, I wonder how this land must have appeared to the earliest people, tramping through the Everglades and discovering alligators, heat, humidity. Did wonder and terror mix easily for them? And then I see kudzu growing on the roadside. Another import, and as much an invading force as any other.

Yeehaw Junction appears. 1-800-4yeehaw, the sign says. "Home to the annual Bluegrass Festival and Fiddle Championship."

Of course I am not really looking, but three birds, shaped like egrets but bigger, brown, with red caps, stand near water on the side of the turnpike. Sandhill cranes, I think! But this is Florida, in the middle of summer. Sandhill cranes are not supposed to be here, are they?

~

2:49 in the afternoon and I'm passing fields of charcoal and ash. Trees completely scorched, partially scorched, grassland all copper, brown, or jet black—acre after acre after acre. Driving down here I heard on the radio that Alligator Alley had been closed due to smoke. Florida wildfires as thick down here as in the western states. And back in Minnesota, I'd looked at the Interagency Fire Maps on the Web a day before I left and seen the West lit up like signal fires in ancient wartime. A friend sent an e-mail from Alaska. Wildfires, she said, are leaping breaks and closing roads. It's a dry, hot summer in North America.

By what mechanism I don't know, the burned area suddenly stops, and trees, the evergreens, the grasses return to green. But the story continues. The fire seems to have jumped the turnpike. First the east, now the west side is scorched copper, black, and brown. A short while later the fire is on the east again and then the west. What wind, I wonder, danced sparks across the pavement?

3:15 in the afternoon and the first exit for Disney World, Universal Studios, Sea World, and beyond them, back on the Atlantic coast, Cape Canaveral.

The jazz station brings me Harry Connick playing "On the Sunny Side of the Street" after a traffic report where they tell me the locations of injury accidents and slow traffic. On the news this afternoon, I learn that a Turkish ship was escorted out of Philadelphia because of a bomb scare, although it may have been a hoax. A high-speed train in Turkey has derailed, killing more than a hundred people. I learn that the 9/11 Commission report blames just about everybody and asks for more cooperation. And I learn more about the ex-Tarzan, whose tiger escaped and was shot by police.

You cannot see Disney World from the Florida Turnpike. Endless townhomes and strip malls, yes. Endless places to start a business, or retire from one, yes. Otherwise just hills, grass, and trees. And I am grateful for this lack of visual noise. Nowhere on the radio news do they talk about the physical world, the planet spinning through space, the accumulation of molecules that make you and me, the fact that the clouds in southern Florida this afternoon provide their own kind of drama.

~

North-central Florida, Interstate 75 heading north. Roadside stands for oranges, grapefruit, pecans, vegetables. National Public Radio brings me news of Europe, the Middle East, and Washington, and an essay about stuffed animals. The highway passes groves of live oak, hung with Spanish moss. It passes cattle farms, radio antennas, billboards for Indian River fruit, and the We Bare All Adult Store: Couples Welcome. The drivers who pass me now talk on cell phones and stare straight ahead. They don't look left or right much. This is the time of day for getting somewhere. Home from work. Away from home. The destination is what's on most people's minds. What clouds there were have dissolved into substantial haze and amber light.

The exit for the Museum of Drag Racing goes by quickly. Fourteen miles south of Ocala, I'm trying to remember why I know that Ocala means horses. Something about the Ocala region is all bound up with riding. Ocala is where the Seminole War started, when Osceola would not be moved away. After Ocala, there's Gainesville and the University of Florida, then the Panhandle, and then Alabama. 4:54 in the evening and I pass under one of the wildlife overpasses. Sign says, "Cross Greenway."

I pass sign after sign for restaurants and hotels where I have never been but know very well. And as the haze in the air thickens I find myself wondering about the comfort there is in knowing what to expect. Why is it we take such comfort in knowing in advance the quality of where we will eat and sleep? Comfort versus—what? Not discomfort. Risk, perhaps? Driving along, I see the hotel advertisements for Fairfield Inns, Courtyard Inns, and Super 8s—you name it. I know in advance what they will look like, the layout of the lobby, whether breakfast is included. Likewise, I see ads for Denny's and McDonald's and Perkins and the Olive Garden. I know their menus. Why is it I will pick one of those instead of Ma and Pa's Roadside Eatery?

Certainly even the earliest ancient travelers returned to places they knew and liked and relied on advice in visiting others. But how often did they also close their eyes in a place untested? How often did they ask for food, unsure at every level, and also grateful it was there?

Have we done away with, or simply lost, a part of the human tradition, the part of the innkeeper? We no longer have innkeepers, it seems. We have desk clerks. We no longer have local food, except as a celebrated oddity. There is a part of me that wishes the chains would go away. That I would find a place, and that the place would be wonderful and unique, and I could tell a story about it in the next town and the town after that. There's a part of me that wishes I would find a place and it would be horrid, and I could tell a story about it in the next place and the place after that.

I turn on my weather radio. There is a storm somewhere. It does not have the characteristics of a tropical cyclone, but it will be monitored. Somewhere in the Atlantic or in the Gulf, a storm is trying to get organized.

What I hear on the radio is also a shift in tone. No longer reported with the intimacy of the Reef Report, the storm is important but almost foreign. It might get here someday, but it is not here now. Somewhere, I don't know where, the psychology of Florida shifts from the Keys and the Atlantic and the Gulf, the coral, the diving, to the exoticness and the danger of Miami, the Cuban community, the spring break mentality of Fort Lauderdale. Somewhere in the center of the state north of Disney World, it shifts again from the Caribbean to the Civil War. It shifts from a history that is external and physical to one that is domestic and political.

The question, Where are you? always has multiple answers. Even if the only answer you're looking for is historical, the possible answers are staggering. Historically, ignoring the earth under the Jeep, this is where I am in my life as an individual human being. This is where I am in the process of my unfolding life. Historically, ignoring my own life and simply looking at this little bit of earth on the interstate highway heading north, this place is rich and complicated. Farms on the west side of the highway—beautiful, black four-board fences bordering each field and surrounding each live oak—give the impression of wealth and good character. But this little spot of land was once Native American land. They spoke a language called Timucua here. According to my National Geographic map of North American Indian cultures, a Franciscan missionary named Francisco Pareja learned Timucuan and wrote the first grammar book of a North American language. But that language is gone. This little spot of land was then Spanish, then part of the expanding United States. And I am fairly certain slaves worked this earth. Then came war. Then came tourism. And throughout it all came the rush of hurricanes off the Atlantic or Gulf coasts.

What do we do with this information today? How bound are we by history? As a northerner and a Democrat driving through this area, do I bring that past to my understanding? Or do I say past is past, let's move on?

On the right side of the highway kudzu is consuming the forest. I go speeding past a policeman. The speed limit is seventy; I'm doing eighty. I'm partially shielded by a truck on my left side, the truck going a little faster than I am, and the policeman comes after neither of us—waiting, perhaps, for the really juicy ticket, the grownup in the Lexus doing 110.

5:30 in the evening. The exits for Gainesville, the University of Florida, and the Museum of Natural History go by. A blue Corvette with a Wisconsin license plate passes me. The license plate reads "Cure E US"—Curious. A young couple rides in the Corvette. The man driving. The woman, absorbed by some book, never looks up.

White egrets share the fields with cows quite naturally. Signs at every rest stop and turnpike service area promise nighttime security. Highway signs remind me that this is an evacuation route.

~

6:20 in the evening and I make the turn onto Interstate 10, enter Suwannee County, now heading west toward Tallahassee. The haze from the sky has lowered to ground level, but isn't quite thick enough to be called fog. I've tucked in behind an eighteen-wheeler, asking his permission on the CB to draft for a while to save me some gas. He laughs and says sure. The sun sets directly in front of us. The forest is thick with pine and kudzu. Pine tree farms line both the north and south sides of the interstate now. Not Christmas trees, perhaps just good lumber. A sign tells me I'm passing the Spirit Suwannee Music Park and Camp. More tree farms, the smell of evergreens thick in the air. It smells like spruce, if my nose is that good.

As I cross the bridge for the historic Suwannee River, the green highway sign shows a bar of music in four-four time—the opening notes of

"Way Down upon the Suwannee River." Also at the bridge, a sign announces the Long-Leaf Pine Restoration Project.

A state trooper, pulled over behind a U-Haul truck disabled on the side of the road, turns off his flashing lights as we pass. I'm following a Budget Rental truck towing a car from South Carolina. The trooper turns off his lights just at the moment when I know he's got us on his radar. He doesn't pull out immediately. I think we're safe, but a few minutes later I see a sedan approaching fast from behind. I'm sure I've had it, but he goes by. He goes by the Budget Rental truck. He goes by the Mayflower moving van in front of that. He passes all three of us breaking the law minutes before. I never see the trooper again.

Interstate 10 west is also a hurricane evacuation route. This is the only route, of course. People from Key West would not flee a hurricane up through the Panhandle of northern Florida. Still, an entire state needs to be ready to move on short notice when the weather says move. And they need the roads to be there when they move. Planning.

7:00 p.m. The sun still ten degrees or so above the horizon. The haze still on the ground and in the air. Driving straight into the sunset through the haze, it's almost as if this day's twilight in northern Florida becomes a kind of dreamtime when the ghosts of the past can get up and walk through your imagination. But not being local, I don't know the stories. So what I see is just green of the landscape and try to imagine those who were here before.

License plates from Tennessee, Missouri, Alabama, Georgia. A cattle truck from Oklahoma. A semi from Maine. I can see there are only two cows in the cattle truck, so on the CB I ask the driver if he's really hauling just two cows from northern Florida all the way back to Oklahoma. "Nope," his answer comes back; "I'm hauling bull." Although nobody keys a microphone, I imagine every trucker in radio range is smiling.

7:31 and the exits for Tallahassee show up. The sun still up in the sky though no longer sharp behind the thicker clouds, the haze has thickened and is already becoming dew on the grass. According to the sign for Cross Creek Place, it's 81 degrees. Light jazz from a station in Tallahassee fills the car. Twilight deepens. A license plate from Michigan. Even at seventy miles an hour, and often more, this is a quiet time on the highway. Miles go past, hours go past. Every field and every hill pleasant, or at least interesting, to look at. But also disconnected somehow from the life inside the Jeep. A pretty picture show that asks for nothing but a witness, and I am happy to see it.

8:35 in the evening. The sun has set and the haze has become fog. Panama City to my left, Pensacola dead ahead. I leave Interstate 10 and turn right, turn north, out of the Panhandle of Florida, toward Alabama on U.S. 231. Thirty-two miles to Dothan, and beyond that—for me tonight—Montgomery. The highway is forested on both sides, the nighttime sky only a shade lighter than the jet black of the trees. I wonder if it's possible these days to drive through a country and not know what it is. A sliver of a crescent moon hangs in the western sky, setting early tonight, its light diffused by the haze. Bugs hit the windshield as fast and hard as rain. No stars at all.

8:55 p.m.—I cross the state line. I am now in Alabama the Beautiful. Seven miles out of Dothan, I pass the site for the National Peanut Festival. I also pass the Dothan National Golf Club and a hot springs resort. A green highway sign on the side of the road announces, mysteriously, "Police Jurisdiction."

In Dothan I stop at a Shell station to fill up the Jeep, and I'm struck by the humidity, the hard weight of the water in the air, and the tremendous sound of the bugs in the woods. The gas attendant, when I walk in to compute my gas mileage, calls me sir. Chamber of Commerce stuff in the gas station lets me know Dothan is the home of the world's smallest city block (it's in the *Guinness Book of World Records*), a giant gold peanut sculpture proclaiming that Dothan is the Peanut Capital of the World (a quarter of the country's entire peanut harvest comes from within seventy-five miles of Dothan), the Future Masters Gold Tournament for junior golfers, the Adventureland Theme Park, and a ten-foot statue of Joseph inscribed with Genesis 37:17: "For I heard them say, Let us go to Dothan" (the original name of the town was Poplar Head). The town motto is Everything in a Nutshell. Outside town, the Visitor Center at the Farley Nuclear Power Plant is temporarily closed.

At night, though, Dothan looks like nearly everywhere else. Traffic lights. Convenience stores and gas stations. Fast food and bars. U.S. 231 north out of Dothan at 9:35 at night is a black ribbon of asphalt that could be anywhere. Trees line both sides, but I can't tell you what kind—dark masses just border the roadway. The wind rises and falls a little bit. The cars, mostly single file, head north and south. I pass a deer on the side of the road which startles me, but I don't seem to bother it at all. The crescent moon does not give off enough light to illuminate the roadway or the trees. Another sign, all out by itself on the highway, says simply, "Police Jurisdiction."

I pass the town of Ozark. Fort Rucker is ten miles to my west, with the U.S. Army Aviation Museum. North of Ozark, light from a strobe on top of something I cannot see, a water tower perhaps, is diffused by the fog and haze so that the entire world pulses with that intense white light. Eerie. I smile, though, at a memory. When I was an undergraduate in Columbia, Missouri, I had a friend who one night thought she was going crazy. The world, she said, was flashing. None of the rest of us could see it until later, but the town had put a strobe on top of a water tower that day, and that night every store window on Broadway was reflecting the flash—ever so slightly.

I know nothing, really, about the mechanics of memory, about the way the chemicals and electrical currents in our brains store and release information. I have not remembered that Columbia story for nearly thirty years. And yet on a dark road in Alabama it comes back to me as fresh and funny as if it were yesterday. I made no decision to bring that story with me on this trip. I made no decision to save it so long ago. But there it is, and I'm happy because of it.

10:15 p.m. and the town of Troy. Troy State University is here. Must be an interesting place, I think. But I am tired, and close enough to the end of this day to push the throttle and rush.

11:18 p.m. Montgomery, Alabama. I pull off the highway at the exit for my hotel. The same exit for the Alabama Shakespeare Festival. So much history here! But not for tonight. I have not seen Alabama this evening except as asphalt and roadway, the occasional face and polite conversation at a gas station. But I will be here in the morning, too, when daylight will show me the shapes of buildings and hills as well as the echoes of history. Tonight, the man at the hotel desk swipes my credit card through his reader and hands me a plastic key card in return. I haul my bag into a room and go to sleep a happy man.

Day Two

Seven o'clock in the morning and Montgomery, Alabama, wakes up to 79 degrees and what feels like 500 percent humidity. The haze and fog, thick on the ground and shining off the Alabama River as I cross on I-65, make the traffic, itself already thick with this morning's rush hour, soft-edged and shimmery. The capital of Alabama is green in the haze.

Hot coffee steams from the mug in the cup holder by my right leg, and the radio brings me the local morning news—people and places and issues I can't begin to recognize. Do I have any idea, any good idea, where I am?

I know the basic history, the schoolbook stuff. And last night, with the computer, I reminded myself of some dates. In 1822 the steamboat *Harriet* pulled into Montgomery and opened trade between here and the Gulf coast at Mobile. In 1835 Dr. James Marion Sims, the "father of modern gynecology," opened a practice here before moving to New York in 1853 and founding the women's hospital. In 1846 Montgomery was selected as the new state capital, and in 1849 the capitol building burned to the ground.

I knew the Civil War began when the Confederate soldiers fired on Fort Sumter in 1861, but I did not know until last night that the orders to do so were telegraphed from Montgomery. I knew that Jefferson Davis was inaugurated as the first president of the Confederate States of America in 1861 and that Montgomery was the first capital of the Confederacy before it moved to Richmond, Virginia, but I did not know that in 1887 the Lincoln Normal School, founded as a private school for African Americans, moved to Montgomery and eventually evolved into Alabama State University. I had no idea that the Wright brothers established a flight school outside Montgomery in 1909, only six years after Kitty Hawk (the site is now Maxwell Air Force Base). And I did not know that Nat King Cole was born here in 1919.

I knew that Rosa Parks refused to give up her seat on the bus in 1955, and I knew that in 1961 the Freedom Riders pulled into Montgomery and were met by violence. I knew that Martin Luther King Jr. became president of the Montgomery Improvement Association in 1956 and in 1965 led the marches to protest voting restrictions. I did not know that in 2000 Rosa Parks was inducted into the Alabama Academy of Honor.

On the highway heading north, I listen to the news and watch the forest and farmland go by, and I wonder what meetings there are between place and history. All these things happened here, but the here of now is nothing like the here of then. We keep the stories. We keep them as part of our social and civic understanding. But how deeply do they remain in our souls?

I have a story from checking in last night and checking out this morning—a story about southern hospitality and charm. It's a very small story. But it is a story nonetheless, and one I'll keep.

Checking into the hotel last night, I tried to get the hotel's wireless modem system to work for my computer, but the system insisted on trying to connect to the network of the hotel next door. That other hotel had a stronger signal, or a better receiver, or something. The desk clerk, however, would not let it go as a simple glitch. He could not fix the problem, but he also could not let me go without sincere apologies and regret. The hotel promised a service and he could not deliver it. In one small way, hospitality had failed—and this troubled him.

Checking out of the hotel this morning, a young black woman, her family waiting for her back in the room, stood in front of the white desk clerk, her folio showing a cash payment that had been posted and then adjusted off. "No," she said, "it should not have been adjusted off." The clerk fell over himself with apologies and kindness, saying he would look into the matter. He would call the other clerk. He'd find a way to make it right. Another young black woman, from the staff, saw me looking at the coffee as she was wiping the counter. I was really just waiting for my turn to check out. She said, "I have a pot back here for you. Couldn't have made it more than ten minutes ago." Pointed to it, smiled, wanted to make sure I was taken care of. I filled my cup, said thank you, stepped back to the desk. An Asian man walked into the lobby, and then a black man. She said the same thing to both of them.

I don't know a thing about the law of oriental hospitality, or why it's in the annotations of my Bible. But once upon a real time, I worked in hotels. There are guests in a hotel, and you take care of your guests.

∾

Interstate 65 is quick out of town—three lanes, seventy-five miles an hour, all of us speeding ever so slightly. It crosses rivers, moves through small forests, pastureland. In the hotel room this morning, I watched the Weather Channel for a little bit. To the north and to the west, rain and strong storms. They said this will be the problem area of the country today. This, of course, is the area the Jeep is now pointed toward.

I may not get far enough today to really hit the storms. Maybe I'll hit them tomorrow morning. Right now, though, watching the southern sun rise over a haze in the middle of Alabama, a long way from my home, a long way from Key West, and a long way from where I'm going, I'm beginning to see that the country is huge.

7:30 in the morning, and I pass a crew of mowers working the median and the shoulders of the highway. Kudzu-covered forests here look like abstract sculptures—half monster, half teddy bear. Off in the distance, a hawk soars. As I move toward Birmingham, I'm moving into the southern end of the Appalachian Mountains.

I pass the exit for the Confederate Memorial Park, and I'll admit I don't know how the people of Alabama do it. How do you take pride in the Confederacy and pride in the civil rights movement at the same time?

And here's another question, more immediate this morning. What is it that makes a landscape beautiful? Why is it that the sight of a calm ocean or the rolling hills of central Alabama fill me with a kind of happiness and a kind of peace? Both landscapes are a long way from the flatland prairie of my home that I also find beautiful.

As I pass the town of Clanton, north on I-65, and pass a water tower in the shape of a peach, I meet a Jeep heading south on the interstate. The driver and I wave at each other, as Jeep drivers do. His Jeep is black, or dark blue, or perhaps dark green, but I know this only from the back. The front of his Jeep, from the hood back past the doors, is covered in the rust-red soil of Alabama.

8:02 in the morning, and I pass the town of—Saginaw? That's a town in Michigan. An electronic highway sign, one of those giant reader boards that spans the highway (out west these are used to give mountain pass and road conditions in winter), reads, "Air quality alert for Friday; reduce your driving." A short while later, another sign over the highway. "Air quality alert today; reduce your driving." Zipping under both signs at seventy miles an hour, I'm not sure how to reduce my driving.

A vanity plate on a car I pass: CIFUKAN—See if you can. Normally I don't care for these license plates, but this one I like. I trust it's a lifestyle and not a silly challenge.

I pass exits for Tuscaloosa and Atlanta, towns that aren't close to each other or to me this morning. But the presence of their names on the same sign over this roadway, the arrows pointing in the direction of the next exit, brings the imagination to those towns at once. We're all connected by modern trails. It's possible to get there from here, and to get there fast.

The south side of Birmingham, rolling green hills, larger than just little swells. These are foothills. There are valleys and cuts and gorges. Nothing around here would claim the name "summit" or "peak," but there are ridgetops. The haze is still thick, but the sun is higher in the sky. The morning traffic isn't too heavy. The radio brings me news from around the world, but my attention really is on the shade of green the summer morning brings to Alabama.

8:31 a.m. and I cross the Birmingham city limits. I can see in the haze the skyline of the city, the downtown area, the high-rises. Here, too, history both clouds and illuminates the city name. Birmingham—site of the 1948 Dixiecrat Convention, which nominated Strom Thurmond for president. Birmingham—site of attacks on the Freedom Riders. Birmingham—site of 1963 bombings, including the one at the Sixteenth Street Baptist Church that killed four children. Birmingham—site of a jail from which Martin Luther King Jr. wrote a letter. Birmingham—birthplace of Condoleezza Rice. Today a green highway sign shows me the exit for the Birmingham Civil Rights Institute.

8:41 in the morning and I turn onto U.S. 78, west toward Memphis, and Birmingham begins to fade behind me. Quickly, though, traffic slows to three or four miles an hour. An ambulance, lights on, sirens sounding, races by me heading east. A police car, lights flashing, races by me heading west. I can see, up in the distance, fire trucks at an inter-section. At the accident site, a sedan is mangled and a dump truck is on its side. Police comfort or attend to a man on his knees by a utility pole. Tough to tell what happened.

U.S. 78 is not an interstate. It brings me by a gas station with an old gentleman out front selling shoes from the back of a black trailer, past stores selling lawn ornaments, TV repair shops, banks, grocery stores, traffic lights. Because it's not an interstate, it's also not nearly as level. It rises and turns and falls and turns again. Back up to speed, sixty miles an hour, the miles go by and the driving is fun. Billboards for churches and the upcoming concert by Cher, her farewell tour. License plates from Oregon, Mississippi, and Minnesota. I pass a white Land Rover, its windows soaped to say "Warriors Rock" and "World Series Bound." I assume it's carrying a Little League softball player. Another window reads "Tyler #7."

U.S. 78 west becomes a six-lane divided highway, speed limit sixty-five. The haze has mostly lifted. There are no clouds to speak of, although the sky is still gauzy. Outside the town of Jasper on a July morning in the northwestern part of Alabama, I'm listening to the London Symphony Orchestra perform Beethoven. What an odd world!

At the exit for Carbon Hill, the divided U.S. 78 ends. It's just a break, a detour around some road replacement, and a cloverleaf exit spins me to the right down onto a local two-lane. On the two-lane through and then west of Carbon Hill, the road meanders. The speed goes from fifty-five down to forty-five and then back up. Truckers on the CB talk about how they just "mosey on through."

∼

There's a man at the Center for Earthquake Research and Information in Memphis named Gary Patterson. I've been trying to get in touch with him. We exchanged e-mails a few weeks ago because I had a question. I'd read that a gravity map would show a "huge cataract" in the Mississippi River south of St. Louis. I'd never heard of this before, and since I was coming this way, I wanted to check it out. So I fired my question to the U.S. Geological Survey, USGS, got bounced from one or two offices, and finally wound up in touch with Gary. I want to talk about this part of the country from a geologist's point of view, I said. What's happening here? I told him I would be looking at landscape and history and a personal look at one giant trip through the country, and he said we could get together for coffee at nine o'clock some morning. I said that considering where I'm starting, 9:00 a.m. isn't going to work. He's been silent ever since then. I called him this morning, left a message. He has yet to call me back.

As I cross the Little New River, the road rises, and a border of trees on both sides makes the highway seem like one long corridor. The sky has gone clear, and puffy clouds have appeared. It is still hot and very humid. I enter the town of Winfield, and a sign tells me that "Winfield is too pretty to litter." The Winfield varsity cheerleaders, another sign tells me, were once national champions. Outside a church, a message board says, "Every home is a school. What do you teach?" A yard sale has many cars in front and around the corner. Kudzu covers trees and fields.

U.S. 78—the sign says "Appalachian Development, Corridor X"—becomes four-lane again just west of Winfield. Endless forests of evergreen, with an orange yellow wildflower growing along the border. It's very pretty. Looking at the forests, I'm reminded of a fantasy I used to have as a small child. On road trips, in the backseat of my parents' car, I'd watch the forests go by and think, If I had a tent and a little cook set, I could wander just a hundred yards or so into a forest like this and disappear forever. Nobody would see me except for the little bit of smoke rising from a campfire. I wouldn't be so terribly far away that I'd be in wilderness; I'd simply be out of place—where nobody would think to look for me. There's nothing extraordinary about a forest that borders a highway. I haven't thought of that wish for thirty years. But I think it has some merit.

10:23 a.m. and corn appears for the first time on this trip.

10:36 in the morning and Mississippi welcomes me. Still the hills and rises, small valleys, and ravines. Still the forests of pine. But behind the trees that shelter the highway, agriculture now. Fields of corn, other crops going by so quickly I can't tell what they are. I cross a stream called Bull Mountain Creek, Cyprus Creek shortly thereafter; Gum Creek right after that. I drive past what I swear is a road-killed armadillo, but I don't know if they've got armadillos here.

At the Tenn-Tom Waterway, cranes offload lumber from barges. Tupelo arrives, the birthplace of Elvis Presley: "He Dared to Rock," the billboard reads. "Roll on Over to Graceland." I pass signs for an Elvis Presley Park, the Elvis birthplace, and the Natchez Trace Parkway. Another dead armadillo on the side of the road. Music in my head. When I cross the bridge over the Tallahatchie River, I'm surprised to learn it's a very short drop. Billy Joe McAllister could have simply swum away.

Forty-five miles outside Memphis my cell phone rings, and it's Gary Patterson. We're meeting for lunch. 12:29 in the afternoon and Tennessee welcomes me.

~

The east side of Memphis is slow, and hot, and not very pretty. With Gary guiding me on the phone, though, I'm quickly into town and then at the University of Memphis. In the shade of huge trees I find his building, set back a bit, and then his office. He's younger than I expected, with short dark hair and an easy smile. His title is information services director, which means that at one level his job is to put up with people like me.

"You get to put up with all the strange people like me who call, eh?" I say as we shake hands and he leads me into his office. One desk, full bookshelves, pictures of his wife, Christy, and his son and daughter, John and Jamie. "Not all of them are strange," he says. "It remains to be seen."

He gives me a big smile, and I like this guy from the start. We do the normal warmup talk, settle into the chairs a bit, and then get going.

I tell him I know the New Madrid story, or at least a part of it. Beginning on December 16, 1811, three huge earthquakes in southeastern Missouri, each of them magnitude 8 or higher, and then literally thousands of aftershocks. Church bells in Boston rang from the movement; people in Washington DC worried. In all probability the quakes were larger than any California quake before or since. For a short time, the Mississippi river flowed backward.

"But can you see any of this?" I ask. "When I look out the window of my Jeep, what should I look for? I mean, Lake Agassiz, where I live . . . "

"That's the old glacial lake?"

"Yeah—you can see the beaches. There are seven beach levels."

"The real problem in talking about the New Madrid seismic zone," he says, leaning back, "is that the features of the fault are very subtle at the surface. The hallmarks are usually mountains and volcanoes. Whereas with an old lake bed, maybe you'd expect not to be able to see it except for some terraces like you mentioned. Here people expect, and scientists too, we expect to see mountains and volcanoes where you have active tectonic, active seismic earthquakes going on all the time. That's why this is so enigmatic."

"But obviously there's an active fault," I say. "The last big earthquake was one of the biggest that people still talk about. I don't have any idea what it would have measured."

"Nobody really knows, but it was really big—somewhere bigger than 7.2, maybe 8.0 magnitude."

"There was that scare—what?—ten years ago. Somebody said the

New Madrid was going to go right away. Said it was going to be bigger than anything out west."

"He predicted in '89, but his prediction was for 1990. Iben Browning."

"Was he here?"

"I don't know where he was from, I think from California. He wasn't from here. We came out against that statement. But there was one scientist in Blue Hill came out supporting him. Now he's running a—he's got some kind of a . . ."

Gary pauses.

"Vegetable stand by the highway?" I offer.

He smiles.

"Tell me," I say. "When I first started trying to chase down the idea of gravity maps showing a waterfall or rapids south of St. Louis, I read a bit about the Reelfoot Rift. That's what this whole area is, isn't it? From here south, a giant rift valley that never really opened. Basically, it's the Mississippi River bed."

"Yeah, but it's much older than the Mississippi River bed."

"Would it be fair to say the rift caused the Mississippi River valley? That drainage occurred because of that fissure?"

"No. But, to some degree, yeah."

"What is some degree?"

"It's a long story. The Mississippi River, as we know it, is only about 12,000 years old. It used to run on the other side of the topographic feature near here called Crowley's Ridge. This is the only hill you'll see heading west after you cross the river until you get up into the Hard Rock Highlands that run close to Hot Springs and Little Rock. The river ran on the other side of that ridge 12,000 years ago, after the Ice Age, and then skipped over. It broke through that topographic barrier, up near Illinois in a place called Thebes Gap 8,000 years ago and then ran way over there at the base of that ridge and then skipped over here to where it's presently at. It meandered . . . "

"There was no event that caused it to change course immediately?"

"No, but I mean, you're going from a realm where you have an incredible amount of sediment in the streams and no real main channel—a braided stream system that just fingered out, like some places in Montana you see now, and then it changed over to a meandering stream that's one big channel that twists and turns like a hose that's been turned on over time. It changed regimes, it changed the amount of sediments in the river—a lot of things that determined how and where it flows. Obviously, the rift . . . You'll often find the rivers that follow the faults. Some of these faults may not move for millions and millions and millions of years."

I pause for a moment and look out the window. "It must be amazing," I say, "to be out in the field—to pick up a rock or look at some cut in a hillside and see the connections, to make the story seem whole. How in the world do you ever explain that?"

"You want nice general tongue grabbers and what's cool about this place."

"To you, then, what is cool about this place? When you look at a map of the United States and, basically, your jurisdiction here, which you described a minute ago as sort of central and eastern U.S., what is it that you see? When I look at my place back up in Minnesota and North Dakota, I see the prairie. But I also see Lake Agassiz, evidence of glaciers, the old mastodons, bison, and all that stuff. Sometimes all I can see is the need to shovel the drive or mow the lawn, but sometimes I can see the T. rex too."

"So you see many things, not just one?"

"Not just one. And driving up here, I passed a couple of hot springs areas and, of course, there's the sulfur springs over in West Virginia. There's a lot of that kind of stuff, not as much as Yellowstone, but there's a lot of that stuff going on. As a geologist and someone whose primary interest is earthquakes or at least of movement of the plates and stuff, what is it you see? Where am I? Where am I as I drive up and head out toward Kansas City tonight?"

"In my world, I'm in a place where large earthquakes have happened where they shouldn't have. The mechanism for large earthquakes in the stable continental interior isn't defined. Our current understanding of plate tectonics says that the plates are rigid. You should only have big earthquakes if they're at the edges, like California and along the coast of South America."

"Hot spots migrate, though." I say. "We still get volcanoes and other stuff in the middle of plates."

"Your hot spots migrate through—it's true, but you still don't see big earthquakes associated with them. You see magnitude 5s and 6s, like in Hawaii. To have a big earthquake, you need a big fault, not just a tube-shaped hot spot. When a hot spot forms, a hot spot can work its way through and maybe warp the surface and cause a big fault. That's one of the theories that's out there for us right now."

"The New Madrid fault is what kind of fault?"

"Well, it's like California. It's a strike-slip fault, but it's a less stiffing and dry strike-slip fault. You would see this relationship. Since the features aren't very obvious at the surface, this map . . . " He pulls a map from his bookshelf and spreads it on his desk. " . . . which is a fact sheet from the USGS, shows that earthquakes have been plied over time. You've got to have a fault to have an earthquake, and a big fault to have a big earthquake. If you map the earthquakes over time, where they cluster are where the active faults are. Here," he says, finger pointing to the circles and dots along the river, "you can see that more than one fault emerges. This is a strike-slip fault on the southern end. This is a thrust fault. There's another strike-slip section up here."

"Right there?"

"More right here."

"I see it."

"Right there. It's a left-stepping, right-lateral strike-slip."

"Which shouldn't be here at all," I say.

"Well, it's OK to have the faults here. There's no problem there, but it means that when we look at earthquake in general and how they happen, we see these big plates sliding around. Fourteen or fifteen major pieces sliding around and bumping into each other. Where you get the earthquakes according to our present understanding is at the edges of those things. You've got faults and weak spots in the continental interiors. We can account for small earthquakes there because, according to this theory, the amount of movement—North America is moving maybe, along the San Andreas fault, maybe forty-five millimeters per year, maximum difference. That's an inch and three-quarters. That's the rate your fingernails grow. Even there, things don't happen overnight. In the San Andreas system, we have a mechanism to explain how often earthquakes happen based on this differential amount of movement from side to side. It's something you can put in an equation. It will tell you how often you ought to have big earthquakes of different sizes.

Let's use that number, forty-five millimeters in California. Here we do the same study. We only see about three millimeters of movement on opposite sides of the New Madrid fault. There's very little stress of accumulation at the surface. That strain is the way we justify earthquakes worldwide right now. How is energy stored in the continental interior is why we're here. It's not just in the United States. You've got India. You've got central Africa. You've got places all over the world that have old rift systems. I should explain—you asked that a minute ago. I want to explain that—the New Madrid rift. Rift means spreading out. The faults I just showed you are currently being squeezed. That's why we're having earthquakes. So, plate tectonics can change over time. The Atlantic rift that you mentioned has turned on and turned off. When it turned off, the continents quit getting farther apart. They started coming together. They slapped together. That's when the Smoky Mountains were formed, when the continents rammed together. Then the mid-Atlantic rift said, "Oh, I'm still alive." It opened up again and pushed the continents out of the park. They started moving again. The New Madrid system was a place, for reasons we don't totally understand, that wanted to be one these new spreading centers, one of these rift systems that spreads out. Plate boundaries . . ."

"Was the plate breaking there, basically?"

"The North American plate was under tensional forces. It was being spread out. So it decided to make this rift system and centered along what's now the Mississippi River, but it failed. Had it succeeded in being a true rift, we'd have an ocean here now heading west. So "rift" is really kind of confusing. Had it succeeded and become a plate boundary, it would have made not just a fault that has a beginning and an end, but another plate boundary that comes back on itself eventually just like the Pacific rim—just a circle. It failed. There are many of those kinds of rifts in North America. We call them aulacogens. It's a geologic term for failed rift systems. The next question is, Why is the energy accumulating here instead of at one of these other rifts? Although they have little earthquakes, it's nothing like here."

"Earthquakes here," I say, "in the middle of the country, in Missouri of all places, seem more like bad writing than good science. You'd never guess it from what you can see."

"This was tied up in myth and fantasy and legend for a long time.

People say the earthquakes could be felt over huge areas here. Smaller earthquakes felt a hundred miles out. Bigger earthquakes felt all the way up to Canada. That's from the newspapers in 1811 and 1895 and 1843. You don't have to go back into those kinds of history books to see these same relationships. We had 17,000 people report a magnitude 4.6 at the Tennessee-Alabama border. It was felt over two hundred miles away for a magnitude 4.6."

"What year was that?"

"It was this last year in Fort Payne, Alabama: 4.6. I can show you dozens of little earthquakes that are felt over ridiculously large areas. You have a 4.6 in California, and you can barely feel it. Probably the next county, at most two counties away."

"It's a little to do with the soil and the bedrock and transmissivity of the earth, isn't it?"

"Yes. But still it doesn't explain—you have to quantify that. How do you quantify that without a large instrumental earthquake to go by in a quantitative way? You can't. All you can do is model and continue to model. Twenty years ago we used the California models because we thought that the only way to go. Then, here we say, "Hey, all this stuff from 1811 in the newspapers was true. People were feeling these earthquakes on the Atlantic seaboard. It's obvious that they were. Hey, we're having little earthquakes now that have been felt in areas like a magnitude 6 in California except these are only 4s. We're having people call me at one o'clock in the morning from Memphis when an earthquake happens a hundred miles away. Those generally turn out to be people in tall buildings or people who live on loose soil. They're feeling the motion. They're not crazy. We thought they were crazy. I thought they were crazy seven years ago. I don't think they're crazy anymore. They're really feeling those events. These things really do happen. To me, they represent one of the last—I hate to be prophetic and say a frontier—but our understanding of why earthquakes happen in stable continental interiors will probably be the next big thing to influence the way we think about how crust of the earth works. We have to have a way to store energy without seeing a manifestation of that energy at the surface beforehand—meaning that strain in simulation. That means there's some kind of pillar, some kind of energy concentrator at depth. Something of a superhard pillar of rock that could be from a very old hot spot or something. I shouldn't say hard. We don't know if it's hard, Silly Putty, or what—some mechanism to store energy and not release all that. These California models say that over time you should have this big an earthquake based on this much movement. If you haven't had that earthquake over a certain period of time, then you're overdue. Here we're faced with a problem—well, you know, we can look at that time period, but what if it was all ready to go before the period we're considering? What if it's already charged up?"

"Do you have any modeling for prediction, any basic hypothesis in math?"

"No, we don't have a way to predict earthquakes."

"You mentioned, a minute ago, people call you at one o'clock in the morning. On your answering machine you have, "If this is an emergency, call somebody else?" When do people call you, and what do they want from you?"

"They want to tell us they felt an earthquake or ask how big the earthquake was."

"So what they're looking for is confirmation that they're not crazy?"

"'Is there going to be another one? Is this a foreshock? What can we expect? We're really worried about earthquake . . .'"

"What do you say when they call up and say, 'I just felt my house shake?' What do you say to them?"

"If I know it's an earthquake, I can tell them that it was probably an earthquake. Most of the time, we say, 'Do you live close to a train? Do you live close to an air base? Is there an interstate in your area?' Trucks, trains, decoupling—happens all the time. Some are sonic booms, especially with the navy. A lot of this is based on experience as well as science. I mean, I've lived here. I've grown up here. In 1976 I felt a magnitude 5 earthquake. It happened about thirty miles away. It amazed me the next day to see in the papers here that we had structural damage to a central facility from a magnitude 5 at that kind of distance. Even then, people said, 'What's going on with that?'"

"In 1976, you had to be seventeen years old."

"I was pretty close to that."

"You're about my age—what, forty-five, forty-four?"

"Forty-three."

"You were very young then, right? You were interested in . . ."

"No, no, I was in a hunting cabin. It didn't strike me again until I got older and went to other places. I said, Jesus Christ, if I felt an earthquake thirty miles away and it did structural damage where I was standing, it should be a big earthquake. But '76 wasn't a big earthquake. That's really getting to the crux of the matter. Vulnerability is more than just about how often big earthquakes happen."

Gary pauses. "None of this is certain, you know."

"What do you mean?"

"I want to make sure that you get this because it's really important that it's what we think. There are different theories out there. Roy Van Arkdale, a professor in the Geology Department, he and Randy Cox, who's also over there, proposed this hot spot migration theory through the central United States. They think a Bermuda hot spot migrated through here. That's why we can see volcanoes and volcano wannabes spread out all over the area."

"Around where? Here?"

"Yeah."

"Other than the springs, what evidence?"

"The crater in Diamond State Park in Arkansas, and there's the Jackson lava domes. They say volcanism doesn't mean that the volcano made it to the surface. That's an excellent question, too. Hot Springs, Arkansas, is close to a place where we see earthquakes, where some of the biggest earthquakes, not the largest earthquakes, but the number of earthquake clusters of sequences have occurred in a place called Enola, Arkansas. It has a signature that looks like a volcanic signature, earthquakes that go deeper and deeper in a straight line. That's heated groundwater. That's easy enough to say, but the real question is, Is that heated groundwater left over from some subduction of the plates, and is it ocean water that's been carried down with tectonic process and is working its way up now, or is that meteoric groundwater that's gone down through cracks, heated up and come back up? Nobody knows. I mean, you'll get lots of opinions. In my thought, nobody really knows why those hot springs are there right now."

"And," he continues, "here's another curiosity. The Appalachians are tens of millions of years older than the Rockies. But, again, you had those plate rift systems to turn on and turn off. They're on about like a 350-million-year clock, so things have happened several times. How many times have the Smokies been formed? Who knows! Why is it, then, that in the Smoky Mountains, on this side of the Smoky Mountains, you get a lot of earthquakes—maybe eighty-three a year. They're all happening beneath the big surface faults. When those mountains were built, the biggest earthquakes were over on the other side. Now the earthquakes are happening here, and in a trend that's parallel to those mountains, but it's much deeper than any of the surface faults go. Maybe we're getting a new mountain range."

"Are people around here—I would imagine most people here are— aware of the New Madrid fault, the way people in California are aware of theirs?"

"No."

"No?"

"No."

We both sit quiet for a moment, my head filled with new mountain ranges, migrating hot spots, Tennessee earthquakes felt in Canada, the river reversing its flow, the truth of nineteenth-century newspaper accounts, and the work of people who bring it all together.

It's time to go, I say. So many miles still to travel today. We stand and shake hands. We talk about some pictures on his shelves, then walk outside. He tells me there are about sixty people working here. A dozen or so are graduate students. Three or four analyze data from the seismic network. There's a guy down the hall who has a completely different project. He monitors movement of the western Antarctic ice sheet. Gary sees me to the door, where I can see the day is still bright and clear and hot.

"So what do you see," I ask, "in the back of your head, when you drive home at night?"

"I see an area that really shouldn't be here," he says, "according to our present thoughts about how the earth works. Seismic elements in a place where they shouldn't be. It's having about two hundred earthquakes a year. There's not much to see at the surface, yet all of the clues are so tantalizing. A lot of them were wrapped in local newspaper articles since the 1800s. It wasn't until we started putting instruments—we've only had real good instruments in this area since 1996 that can do three-dimensional locations where earthquakes form all the way around. I'm getting to work with great people who are very smart, and maybe we're putting together one of the puzzles of the earth."

Gary hands me a University of Memphis folder with some USGS publications, and when I get to my car I open it and look over them. I read about shake maps—ways to show the extent of damaging shaking after an earthquake—and I read about a fault in India that's much like the New Madrid. I read about the 1811–12 events, the riverbank mudslides, the tremendous upstream wave, the "retrograde current," islands that disappeared, falls or rapids that suddenly appeared, flatboats being swept among it all. I read about the earth suddenly spouting hundreds of geysers of sand and "black liquid." I read about Native American legends of earlier quakes, and I read how dating of "sand blows" and "liquefaction features" gives evidence of events, just as big, in the year 1450 and the year 900.

Looking up and then out the Jeep window, I see robins, people walking, cars on errands. I turn on the radio and hear an ad for some Beale Street bar. "Home of the Blues. Birthplace of Rock and Roll." And as much as I'd like to go there, I feel as if I'm on a different planet. And then I remember a bit from the warmup conversation.

"With all the equipment here," I said, "You actually do get to see the whole planet. If Anchorage shakes today, you're going to know about it," I say.

"We'd know, yeah," Gary said. "We wouldn't go there because they have plenty . . . " And then he paused. "Well," he said, smiling, "we might go."

~

3:09 in the afternoon. Memphis traffic is slow, painfully slow, as I'm waiting to join I-55 north toward St. Louis. A couple of hours in Gary's office. Soon I'll be in Missouri.

The drive up Interstate 55 will take me near New Madrid, Missouri, where I should stop, but I have this feeling in my gut that says, "Hit the road. Get back up to speed before the light fails, see the way the hills are shaped today." There's a part of me that wants to run over to the bridges south of Cairo, Illinois, to see where the Ohio and the Mississippi meet. I've been there before, a long time ago. One bridge over the Ohio, a mile of flatland pavement and then another bridge over the Mississippi. A highway weigh station in between, and a great view of the joining streams. Just off the road there's a state park, and a fort that never became as important as it should have been. I remember driving that road and pulling over for just a moment. I stood there and listened to birds and watched the slow force of water heading south. That was twenty years ago, maybe more. It's a moving place if you imagine what passes those few square miles—how much water, how much history, how much commerce, how much dream and imagination. But I'm in Memphis later than I want to be, and I have promises to keep, many miles to go before I sleep.

I cross the bridge over the Mississippi River. An old-style riverboat goes up the river to my left. "Welcome to Arkansas: the natural state. Buckle up for safety," the sign says. Somewhere underneath me, the bridge is being retrofitted to the tune of more than $100 million for when the next big earthquake comes. On the west side of the river are row crops of some sort, short green bushes—couldn't tell you what. Center-pivot irrigation. Tomatoes, maybe? They're about that size. Vestiges of kudzu hang on the fence line. A license plate from Minnesota. A strong press on the accelerator and the Jeep nearly flies north on 1-55.

4:23 p.m. and I cross into Missouri: the Show Me state. This is where I was born, though more than five hours west. This is the state where I went to college, the state where I met my wife and the state where we were married. This is the state where my parents live, and my sister too. This is a state where I have stories. Stories that include friends and family and lovers. Stories that include the Highway Patrol. But this is not a state that speaks the word *home* to my soul.

It may not be possible to go home again, but it's certainly possible to leave. It is possible for a new place, in my case the northern prairie, to steal your heart so completely that the old stories simply echo.

Hazy sky, some clouds, still the row crops on both sides of the road. This is flatland, river-bottom driving. The radio tells me there are thunderstorms, some of them strong, many of them building, in the north and west distance, but there is no evidence of them here. Catfish farms appear on the east side of the highway. The corn is nearly all brown, ready for harvest. A severe thunderstorm warning comes from the radio. I don't see the clouds, but I do see a haze that would make them invisible. The weather radio tells me that winds of sixty miles an hour and nickel-size hail are in this storm. The exit for New Madrid goes by without so much as a quiver.

There is a drama, though. "All Things Considered" on NPR is inter-rupted by the weather reports. The haze resolves itself into cloud shapes, white and black and roiling in the angled afternoon sun, the leading edge of the system I'm rushing into. The sky darkens quickly. Cars in the oncoming lanes now have their lights on. I cross a bridge for St. John's Bayou and then drive through the town of Miner. The CB tells me I-55 is backed up, but I'm not sure where. Truckers are talking about the wind and about taking alternative routes.

I cross Ramsey Creek and find the storm has already moved to the east side of the roadway. The pavement is wet. The road goes through a small range of hills. Behind the storm, the sky is hazy again. Spray paint on the pillar of a bridge says, "Trust Jesus."

It's late July and some fields here have already been harvested. The interstate enters the rolling hills of southern Missouri. Trees are no lon-ger primarily evergreen. Now there are oaks and who knows what else. The soil is no longer red. Just a few hours ago in the history of this day I was in the South, and now I am in the Midwest. Just a few hours ago, my wonderings were closer to Alabama than home. But the day has changed. There have been earthquakes and thunderstorms and the Mis-sissippi flowing north. It's a different feeling from just a couple of hun-dred miles away. It's a different part of the world and a different part of the earth. The more I go north the corn is less brown, fewer crops are harvested, although corn becomes and more and more the only crop that's seen from the highway. The sun is out; the weather has passed. The radio brings symphonies and news, commentary on political par-ties here and abroad. All sorts of things are possible.

Seven o'clock in the evening. The sun is setting in the western sky. The highway begins to cut through the hills—exposed rock on the right and left. I'm reminded of the conversation earlier this afternoon. Just under here, in the bedrock, are some of the oldest rocks. These hills used to be part of the Appalachians. Who knows how many times they were formed? It's amazing what you see when you look hard enough. It's amazing what you can look for if you ask the right questions. I pass the exit for the Ulysses S. Grant National Historic Site.

～

8:20 in the evening. On the west side of St. Louis, under a hazy and humid evening sky, thick traffic follows an exit and suddenly I'm on

I-70, crossing a bridge over the Missouri River. The water seems nearly metallic in this light. City, all around. Two hundred years ago, this same spot, or somewhere near, saw the start of something extraordinary. On May 14, 1804, William Clark wrote in his journal: "Set out at 4 oClock p.m. in the presence of many of the Neighbouring inhabitents, and proceeded on under jentle brease up the Missourie."

Today, though, as I cross the bridge, the feeling is different. A sign tells me the ozone forecast is green. Breathe easier. Traffic slows to a crawl in front of some accident, red lights flashing in the distance; a police cruiser races by on the shoulder. All of us have our windows up. Radio news is not encouraging.

I pass another sign that tells me I'm at the beginning of the nation's first interstate highway. Here! Here, I think. Here, there should be a monument, or a shrine, or at the very least a museum. There should be some history of the American road, from deerpath to scramjet. And yes, I know what I'm saying. I'm not excusing gridlock, road rage, the wasted oil, the obscene consumption of gasoline. I'm not celebrating the anonymity of the people or the violence to the earth or the profound ugliness of so much of our roads. But the very idea of it all, the scope of the desire, is astounding.

1956, the sign says. But the date says nothing about the hope, which began much earlier. It was in 1938 that FDR's administration undertook the first study to see if the superhighway system was possible. Section 13 of the Federal Highway Act of 1938 reads, in part, "The Chief of the Bureau of Public Roads is hereby directed to investigate and make a report of his findings and recommend feasibility of building, and cost of, super highways not exceeding three in number, running in a general direction from the eastern to the western portion of the United States, and not exceeding three in number, running from the northern to the southern portion of the United States, including the feasibility of a toll system on such roads." And this single sentence is itself an echo. President Thomas Jefferson wrote to Meriwether Lewis that, "The object of your mission is to explore the Missouri River, and such principal streams of it, as, by its course and communication with the waters of the Pacific Ocean, whether the Columbia, Oregan, Colrado, or any other river, may offer the most direct and practible water-communication across the continent, for the purposes of commerce."

Here, I think. But even here, I know, isn't quite real. Lewis and Clark had come a long way already, just to get here so they could start. And so many years later, on June 29, 1956, Missouri was the first state to issue contracts under the government's new highway funding. The first contract went to a portion of U.S. 66. But that road and that work were already under way. On August 2, Missouri gave a contract for this section of I-70, which became the first project started fresh. Here, back then, was just a line on a contract. But soon enough the equipment showed up, the men moved in, the earth was turned, and away we went.

We were, had been, and remain, as William Clark said on the morning of their beginning, "fixing for a Start."

The traffic clears and I-70 becomes two ribbons of lights. One white, one red; one traveling toward me, the other traveling away. The sun has set. The crescent moon is a little bit higher in the sky, but nonetheless it still chases the sunset. City land falls away and farmland takes over, but there are still too many people here for this to be rural. Too many billboards for this to be lonely road.

At 9:16 I'm approaching Kingdom City and a story that makes me smile. The story, as I learned it first, is wrong. What I was told happened simply didn't. But the story was absurd enough to stick. Once upon a time, I was told, during the Civil War, there was a county in Missouri, Callaway County, that decided to secede from the North as well as the South and set up an independent monarchy. The Kingdom of Callaway. So this is what they did, and it lasted about a month before the Union troops showed up to change their minds.

The truth is not so far from this. In October 1861, Union General John B. Henderson was moving west toward Callaway. In Callaway, Confederate Colonel Jefferson F. Jones was not happy with the idea. But men from the county had already gone to fight, for both the North and the South, and there was no one to defend the land. Jones had logs painted to look like cannons, and, perhaps remembering George Washington, he kept extra fires burning at night to give the impression of a force much larger than his remaining old men and young boys. And he made sure the Union side heard the rumors of the force. Henderson was fooled, to the point of negotiating a treaty. He promised not to invade Callaway as long as Jones promised not to invade the United States of America. And so the Kingdom of Callaway was born from a military deception. But even here, things aren't so simple. Colonel Thomas J. C. Fagg, the man under Henderson, ignored the treaty the very next day. Still, like the birth and surrender of the Conch Republic, the Kingdom of Callaway makes a good story.

Too many stories on this road, for me. In Fulton, I pass Westminster College and the Winston Churchill Memorial. In this small town in Missouri, at this small college, Churchill first used the term "iron curtain" in a speech.

Lewis and Clark. The interstate highway system. The Kingdom of Callaway. Winston Churchill. This is the highway where my father once hit a deer with his car. This is the highway that leads to home.

At ten o'clock in the evening I'm on U.S. 54, coming in on the east side of Jefferson City. The capital of Missouri. My wife's hometown. How do I pick the stories to tell when every mile holds another memory? There used to be a drive-in movie theater here, where I would stop to rest on the trip between my parents' house and my college apartment, sitting on a hillside next to my car, watching the screen and listening to the sound coming from all the idle sound boxes hanging on poles. My wife's parents used to live here at the top of a hill, and our children used to swim in their pool. Wonderful summer days. Are these enough?

Two bridges cross the Missouri River at Jefferson City. When I learned this road, there was only one. When I learned this road, on the east side of the river there used to be a small town named Cedar City. It was the place Lewis and Clark named Cedar Island, after the American red cedar tree. But floods and highway improvement have removed the town completely. Even though the drive-in theater is gone and Cedar City is only the story of an old exit, and even though U.S. 54 in front of me remains four-lane when in the past it dropped to two, this is a familiar drive, one my hands and feet know well. In front of me, the farmland of central Missouri, and then the hills of the ancient Ozarks. Then the Osage River, which Zebulon Pike ascended on his way to Pike's Peak. And then the horrific electric gaudiness of the Lake of the Ozarks. But then, happily, the open door of my parents' home. I press on the gas.

Day Three

7:49 in the morning. U.S. 54 heading east through Osage Beach on my way out of Lake of the Ozarks and the morning is gray, overcast, much colder than I expect for the end of July. On the radio I learn that temperatures this morning are in the sixties, with highs expected to be only in the middle seventies.

This is not a road I enjoy. Four lanes wide, with a center turning lane, the pavement is almost wide enough to handle the summer crush. Pickup trucks. Trucks pulling boats. Sports cars. Sedans. Every family bringing their kids for a weekend at the lake. Every high school and college kid looking for sun, water, and action. This is tourist central. The Lake of the Ozarks is really just the dammed-up Osage River, but ocean racing boats are the rage among those with too much money, or at least too easy credit. Loudness, in all its personal and physical definitions, is the apparent rule. There was a time, in the once upon a time, in my and my parents' youth, when you could water ski here in glass smooth coves. There was a time when you could boat here without wondering what rocket was going to run you down. But such days are rare now. On the road this morning, there is very little traffic. It's early, and cold, and the air holds a misty drizzle. The go-cart tracks are still empty. The bumper boats are yet to be started. The shopping center is not open. An officer of the Missouri State Water Patrol hauls his own boat toward a landing.

As I pulled away from my parents' home this morning, I saw a few souls already playing golf, but nobody on the strip is playing miniature golf. The kids in hotels, rented condos, and rented homes are still asleep or whining about being awakened. As I cross the Grand Glaize bridge, only three or four boats are out motoring on water already choppy in this morning's wind. When I crossed last night, I could see the red, green, and white lights of maybe two dozen.

This is not a road I enjoy, but it's a road I know well. And this morning its miles fall away under my tires with my thoughts somewhere else. Last night I learned my father has a cancer.

Not even a week ago, on my way down to Key West to start this trip, I sat with my parents in a Kansas City hotel room while my father took laxative pills to get ready for a colonoscopy. In the past few months he'd become anemic, and no one was really sure why. The colonoscopy was going to look for a problem in the intestines. Somewhere in the back of my head I knew there might be trouble, but my father has always been extraordinarily healthy. I was certain the test would be negative, and some wonder vitamin would bring the iron levels in his bloodstream back into line.

Last night, though, we had the report. We knew on the day of the test that there was something there that shouldn't be, but the report, pictures included, gave the details. From the Description of Findings:

> Informed consent was obtained . . . no contraindications were noted on physical exam. . . . Immediately prior to sedation for endoscopy the patients ASA Classification was Class 1: Healthy patient, no medical problems. . . . The procedure was performed with the patient in the left lateral decubitus position. . . . The patient tolerated the procedure well. There were no complications. The heart rate was normal. The oxygen saturation and skin color were normal. . . . In the proximal ascending colon, a nonobstructing, large-size, fungating, friable mass was seen. There was stigmata of bleeding from the mass.

And then under a section called Additional Comments: "The mass lesion in the cecum likely explains his anemia and is probably a cancer. He will need surgical removal of the lesion." Also on the report: "He has had a CT of the chest and of the abdomen that are negative for suggesting metastases."

In the kitchen last night, reading the report, looking at the color pictures of the inside of my father's colon, we knew surgery was the next order of business. But there was some question about timing. It could be in one week. It could be in three. We wouldn't even know this much for another four days.

In three weeks, my parents said, you could be to the north shore and back, easy. If it's one week, I said, I could always turn around. "There's nothing to do between now and then," my father said. "I have cancer—they are going to try and cut it out. From now to then there's no use just sitting around." Press on, they said. So, not knowing what else to do, in the morning I poured coffee in my mug and turned the key in the Jeep's ignition, repeating to myself over and over: "If it's one week, I can always turn around."

∼

Once past the turnoff for Bagnall Dam, the wall that holds back the Osage and creates the lake, the reason for even more miles of souvenir and saltwater taffy shops, the strip malls fall away. The rolling hills of the Ozarks come back to the roadside. The Osage River itself, brown, muddy banks, flows under the bridge. The forests are green again, despite the thousand billboards for realtors. Some place, I think. Old river. Ancient hills. Cheap thrills. Even at this hour, a fair number of cars head west on U.S. 54 for a weekend at the lake, despite the blanketing gray clouds.

I don't know if there will be storms in these clouds today, but I know I'm heading toward where the forecast says it will be the wettest and the windiest. In Eldon, I exit U.S. 54, then turn on Highway 52 and head toward Kansas City. Just off U.S. 54, the road is wet from recent rain. Everybody is driving with their lights on. Then suddenly, heading west on 52, I drive through downpour cells and then gentle rain and then downpour again, rain so hard my wipers on high cannot keep up. Cows continue to graze in the fields on both sides of the roadway, however. The corn continues to grow. And it occurs to me that even though I've seen lots of cows, and lots of bad weather, I have never seen a cow running for cover.

Highway 52 is just a single ribbon of asphalt, meandering, rising, falling as the topography allows. Election signs for the local state representative and the tax collector dot the roadside. In front of one farmstead there's a sign, "For Sale, George and Ebie." I'm sure George and Ebie are real estate agents, but the sign, at sixty-five miles an hour, makes it look as if George and Ebie are for sale. I smile as I wonder what they'll bring.

The town of Barnett arrives, population 207, and the speed limit goes down to forty-five. The highway passes an Amoco station and a few small homes. Then in a hundred yards or so the speed limit goes back up to sixty and the town is behind me. Hay bales dot the fields to the north of the highway. And then a yellow highway sign that says, "Share the Road," showing an Amish buggy being pulled by a horse.

I have never seen an Amish buggy on the road, except on television, and I do not know any Amish people. But I remember reading about them. The plain people, they call themselves. Romans 12:2 says be not conformed to this world, and somehow that means buggies, a simpler and yet harder farm life. No education after the eighth grade. A separation from the world that makes them a close and closed community, and thus the object of many people's wonder and curiosity. Interesting furniture. They believe pictures are graven images, but they also believe there are exceptions. They don't live without electricity. They just don't like a lot of it.

And also nearby, I know, are the Mennonites, who did not think Martin Luther was radical enough, who oppose war and value experience as a kind of grace. I know a few Mennonites, and I admire them greatly. And since this is Missouri, right in the middle of the Bible belt, I know I'm never more than one house away from the Southern Baptists, who are, well, energetic. And then there are the huge number of Catholics, the Lutherans (mostly Missouri Synod), the Presbyterians, and the Jews. It's a state where religion matters, and often matters loudly.

The Jeep splashes hard through a roadside puddle, and I smile as I remember a line from one of the Cannonball Run movies. "The Missouri Highway Patrol is on a mission from God." More than once, when I was in college, the Missouri Highway Patrol took offense at my interpretation of the speed limit. More than once, I had no excuse other than that speed was fun. There is a story I like to tell about what was supposed to be the first date between Maureen, my wife, and me. This was in Columbia, Missouri. Both of us were students at the University of Missouri. I called her late one night and asked if she would like to go out for a while. She said yes. I lived a few miles north of town and wanted to get into town as fast as I could. The officer said I was driving 103 miles an hour in a 55 mile zone. And, he said, I had a suspended license. I had to call Maureen, and break the date, from a holding cell in the jail while I waited for friends to bail me out.

The most popular election sign this morning is "Chip for Rep." There's a bunch of text on the sign that's too small for me to read as I speed by, but I do know that Chip wants to be a rep.

I continue to drive through torrent and mist, and I almost miss the intersection with Highway 5. Turn right and on my left there is a small Mennonite restaurant, a couple cars out front even this early on a Saturday morning. The sky becomes a more uniform gray, and the rain no longer alternates between drizzle and downpour. My wipers are set on high. It's a hard-rain morning.

Highway 5 crests a hill, and I can see that we're north of the Ozarks. Rolling farmland now, with poplars and oaks. The rain continues strong and steady, though I can see some distance through the soft-focus air. If there is a visual definition of the word "pastoral," I think, it's the sight from Highway 5 looking west over American farmland on a rainy morning. Election signs for state treasurer and governor. Election signs for Sheriff. Elect Gump for sheriff. The Gump sign is orange red with a large black star behind the *G* for Gump.

In Tipton, a town with a round water tower painted like an eight ball, I pick up U.S. 50, which joins Highway 5 for a few miles. West of town, however, Highway 5 turns north, leaves U.S. 50, and passes under a small bridge. And even though I continue west on U.S. 50, my mind, at least for a short while, follows Highway 5. I've driven that road before. I know the road crosses some beautiful small hills, and often on each side there are square plots of ground marked by chain-link fence and military signs. Nuclear missile silos planted with the corn.

The rain comes down harder. The wipers are on high. The speed falls to forty-five miles an hour. This is a warm front moving through the middle of the country, long days of steady rain. This is nothing like the thunderstorm cells so common here. Nothing like the green-sky tornado weather that makes the very air electric.

Nine o'clock in the morning and I turn on the radio for the first time. My choices are Bruce Springsteen, *Car Talk*, country music, or a symphony by Franz Joseph Haydn. Each press of a button and I'm amazed at how the character of the day changes with the other voices brought into the interior of the Jeep. The somewhat lonely sound of rain against the windshield and rooftop, the sound of water under the tires. They take on an entirely different meaning when moving from foreground to subtext. I listen to Haydn for a minute, then switch to *Car Talk*. It's a gloomy morning and my father has cancer. Stories, stories about intractable problems, and humor as the solution seem perfectly right.

The Jeep motors into the town of Sedalia, old brick homes on a beautiful Broadway lined with old, magnificent oaks. The Missouri State Fair is held here. A tornado once tore the west side of town to ribbons. I've stopped here a thousand times, at drive-ins and gas stations, and been to the fair once or twice. But the most poignant memory I have of this town actually took place in Amherst, Massachusetts. I was in graduate school, and also working at a hotel as the night auditor and desk clerk. Set mostly in Missouri, a TV movie called *The Day After* dramatized the aftermath of nuclear war. Jason Robards, wandering about the desolation after the strikes, asks someone about Sedalia. I don't remember who he asked. But the answer, "There is no more Sedalia," caught me off guard on my stool behind the hotel desk. Sometimes, when people ask, "Where would you live if you could live anywhere?" an old home in Sedalia is what I imagine. I don't know a soul in this town, and I know nothing about what it's really like to live here. But if exteriors can provide at least a hint of the life behind the doorway, then there is something good here.

9:29 in the morning and I pass an ambulance and police cars on the eastbound side of the highway. Three or four cars, a few of them facing the wrong direction, have spun out in the rain. Five miles ahead of me is Whiteman Air Force Base, home of the B-2 stealth bomber. Then the town of Knob Noster. Flat, gray sky, steady and often heavy rain. Sometimes a flooded roadway.

~

10:18 in the morning and Kansas City arrives in a rain so thick I can't see more than two-tenths of mile on either side of the road. Every passing car and truck sends plumes of spray and grit hard against my windshield. Charlie Parker on the radio now. And I'm not really looking at road signs. This is the town where I was born. This is the town where my father was born, where my grandfather settled after leaving Denmark and started a dairy farm. His farmhouse, once the center of the Morningview Dairy, now sits as the architectural oddity in the Morningview subdivision—homes my father built on his father's property. Too many stories. Friends and lovers and adventures roll together as easy memory in this morning's rain. This is the town where my mother was once a member of the Kansas City Ballet Guild's board of directors and chair of the annual ballet ball, where she hosted Mikhail Baryshnikov. This is the town where my brother once bought a revolving red light for the top of his car and used it to pull over pretty girls and ask their names.

I never lived here, really. My parents moved to the suburbs of Chicago when I was two, and I had left for college when they moved back. But I visited a lot, and college friends came from here too. So there are days when I feel like every intersection should have a historical marker, and there are days when I feel outside of anything real.

I take an odd way through town. Exit onto State Line, zip over to Ward Parkway, stop for a fast cup of coffee with a friend named Nancy I haven't seen in twenty years, to meet her husband and kids. (I introduced her to her first husband—a relationship that didn't last.) What do you say after twenty years? It felt like no time has passed at all. The cadence of give and take still fast and syncopated and fun. But so far still to go, I said. So far, this day, to make it home.

When I cross the Missouri River again north of Kansas City it is almost noon. In this rain streets are mostly flooded, large spouts erupting from every passing car and bus, traffic is slow, a handful of accidents. It's impossible to make any good time. It's impossible to see the landscape. Somewhere near here, two hundred years ago, William Clark wrote in his journals, "I observed a great number of *Parrot queets* this evening." The note in my edition of the journals says the birds were Carolina parakeets, which are now extinct. Two days later he wrote, "To Describe the most probable of the various accounts of this great river of the Kansas, would be too lengthy & uncertain to insert here." Too lengthy and uncertain. What a wonderful phrase, I think, near the middle of the country. All at once I can see freight trains, commuter cars, semis, and airplanes. Everything and everyone, it seems, in the process of going someplace else fast. How far, I wonder, are we from Sergeant John Ordway, part of the Corps of Discovery, who wrote in his journal here, "I went out hunting 2½ miles & passed a fine Spring Running from under the hills. I drank hearty of the water & found it the best & coolest I have seen in the country."

A license plate from California. A license plate from Alaska. A license plate from New York.

I cross the Little Platte River, and the rain begins to subside, the clouds to lift just a little, but the radio tells me the gloom will continue. When I-29 north crests hills, I can see miles into the distance. Rolling hills. Farmsteads. Crops and cattle. I try, but fail, to reimagine it all, to see it without the centuries since Lewis and Clark and Sergeant Ordway. Too lengthy and uncertain.

I pass a car with a Colorado license plate, and laugh out loud because of a story Nancy told me less than an hour ago. I'd been telling her some road-trip stories, and she then told me one of her own. "It was Christmas break, 1977," she said. "I was a junior in high school. My best friend

Peg, her boyfriend Tim, and I headed to Aspen to stay with a guy I knew from Colorado. He was a ski instructor. Now he is an actor. For a while he was a steward for an airline. He looked like Robert Conrad in *Wild Wild West*. I'd never been to Colorado in the winter. Tim drove some little foreign-made car with a stick shift, and since I think I still hadn't learned to drive, he and Peg traded the driving duty. I was the only one who'd ever been to Colorado, so I was in charge of the map."

"Unfortunately," she continued, "I overlooked one very important factor. Independence Pass on 82 is closed during the winter, completely impassable because of snow. We made it to a fifty-foot tall wall of snow that blocked the road, with a little metal sign hanging from a chain strung across the road that said "closed." So we turned around and headed back down the mountain, on the ice, without chains or snow tires. When the car spun out, all I remember is the feeling in my stomach and the sound of Peg's screaming. It wasn't until the car stopped—I think it was at least five rotations, but that may just be my memory exaggerating—stuck in about five feet of snow in a ditch off the road, that we saw the other side of the road, which for some reason we didn't spin toward, was a sheer drop of—oh, I don't know—*five miles*. We all started shaking. I think Tim threw up. So there we were, at about five o'clock in the evening, on a mountain on a closed road, stuck in a ditch. No blankets, no flares, no food. I think we had a bottle of Jack Daniels. Then a few minutes later, literally, around the corner comes a truck. The driver was a fat old guy in coveralls who said something like, "What the hell are you kids doing up here?" He turned his truck around, pulled our car out of the ditch with a chain, and followed us all the way down the mountain. There was a bumper sticker on his truck that read, 'I'd rather be fishing.'"

Road-trip stories are almost always adventures. We record the beautiful and the unexpected as well as the threats and the things that nearly kill us.

I'm wondering why some stories stay with us and some don't, when the clock reads 12:30 p.m., the rain clouds are breaking up, and the Jeep motors into St. Joseph, Missouri. The stories that stay with us! This place, I know, was the beginning of the Pony Express. I don't know if this story still finds its way into the dreams and wishes of young boys, but I do know there were many nights when I wondered what it would be like to leap on a horse and take off hell bent for the West. The Pony Express only lasted a bit more than a year, from April 1860 to October 1861. 1,966 miles from St. Joseph to Sacramento. Ten days was the normal trip; horses changed every ten to fifteen miles, riders changed every seventy-five to one hundred miles. Riders were paid $100 a month and had to weigh less than 125 pounds. The route was from Missouri, through Kansas, through Nebraska and Colorado and Wyoming and Utah and Nevada before ending in California. The fastest trip was seven days and seventeen hours. The mail on that trip was Abraham Lincoln's Inaugural Address.

As a business, the Pony Express was a failure. As an idea, however, as one of the true stories we save, it hit one of the deeper chords. That image, the young man on the galloping horse, carrying the news into the wilderness and running from danger, is one of the ways we see ourselves. I smile, because in 1866 the Pony Express company was sold to Wells Fargo. Wells Fargo is the name on my checkbook and credit card. So far away, I think. And in my back pocket too.

St. Joseph is also the home to the Stetson hat company, and the town where Jesse James settled and became a family man before Bob Ford shot him in the back of the head. And St. Joseph is the town where my children first ate at a Sonic Drive-in restaurant.

North of St. Joseph, green hills and breaking clouds. Fields of corn. Signs on highway posts for the Lewis and Clark Trail. John Williams and the Boston Pops performing the *Star Wars* music on the radio, filling the car and drawing the imagination up, off the rain-soaked roadway, through the clouds, to the Hubble Telescope and the International Space Station. Perhaps, I think, the dream of the young man on the galloping horse has simply changed to the dream of the young man on the galloping rocket. I have an appointment later today, still several hours in front of me, in South Dakota, and outer space. So many times on this road I've passed a sign: EROS Data Center—Earth Resources Observation Systems. Another part of the United States Geological Survey. Satellites looking back at the earth, looking hard, and then beaming that information to the Dakota prairie. Just as I'd done for Memphis, I'd made a call not long ago and asked if I could visit. It would be late on a Saturday, I said. A man named Dennis Hood said sure.

1:33 in the afternoon and I'm passed by a man I know, who lives in my hometown! I honk the horn and try to wave, but he and his wife are making time and are soon far in front of me. Wild turkeys at the tree line east of the highway. On the west side, a billboard for the Strategic Air and Space Museum. 1:41 and the border of Iowa. Tall fields of corn on the eastern side. The radio brings me the sound track for the Broadway production of *Into the Woods*.

~

I have this wish. I wish it were possible, just once, just for a moment, to see the whole picture. To see how the stories meet, or come close. Maybe this is just a wish to be a historian. Maybe it's a wish to be God. Whatever it is, every new story adds a layer, and every new layer flavors the ones I already know.

2:30 in the afternoon and I'm pulling back onto the highway after stopping for gas on the south side of Council Bluffs. From here, William Clark wrote,

> Capt. Lewis and my Self walked in the Prarie on the top of the Bluff and observed the most butifull prospects imagionable, this Prarie is Covered with grass about 10 or 12 Inch high, (Land rich) rises about ½ a mile back Something higher and is a Plain as fur as Can be Seen, under those high Lands next the river is butifull Bottom interspersed with Groves of timber, the River may be Seen for a great Distance both above & below meandering thro: the plains between two ranges of High land which appear to be from 4 to 20 ms. apart, each bend of the river forming a point which Contains tall timber, principally Willow Cotton wood some Mulberry elm Sycamore & ash. the groves Contain walnut coffeenut & Oake in addition & Hickory & Lynn.

What I see is industrial parks, asphalt, fast food and gas stations, and the urban towers of Omaha, Nebraska.

This is where the Mormon Pioneer Trail crosses the river. This is the place William Clark named in honor of a good meeting between the Corps of Discovery, the Missouri, and the Otoe tribe. In the soil here (and as far away as Louisiana) is the fallout from the Yellowstone super volcanoes 2 million and also 630,000 years ago. Just 20,000 years ago, the glaciers were melting, and the Missouri River filled everything. Always shallow, the river made giant silt flats that dried, then were picked up by the prairie winds and turned into the loess hills. Expensive homes now line the tops of the bluffs.

Western Iowa in midsummer is corn. Corn to every horizon. Yellow wildflowers dot both sides of the highway. The clouds have finally broken up, and under the blue sky my Jeep now throws a shadow on the highway. It's a pastoral and pretty and comfortable vision. It's also hypnotic. A hundred miles go by, maybe more, with nothing more surprising than the sudden yellow green smash of some large bug on my windshield. Every song on the radio, it seems, I've heard too often.

But I still have this wish. South of Sioux City, near the Port Neal landing, are the Lewis and Clark State Park and the Keel Boat Exhibit. And there is my own history of being stranded in blizzards here, with my family. And even here there is also the odd and the unexpected. 74 million years ago, something from outer space crashed into the earth just east of here, near the town of Manson. Something big. People digging wells found rocks that didn't fit, so other people began to pay attention. In 1953 they thought it was cryptovolcanic, a crater formed by the explosive eruption of volcanic gas. In 1966 they decided the crater was an impact site. And for a short while scientists wondered if this could be the site of the big one, the event at the end of the Cretaceous period when all the dinosaurs died. In 1994 they discovered that the dates were off, and the crater was too small.

In Sioux City I pass the exit for Sergeant Bluff, the burial site of the only person from the Corps of Discovery who died. Sergeant Floyd died of a ruptured appendix. On August 20, 1804, Clark wrote, "This Man at all times gave us proofs of his firmness and Deturmined resolution to doe Service to his Countrey and honor to himself after paying all the honor to our Deceset brother we Camped in the mouth of *floyds* river about 30 yards wide, a butifull evening."

On the north side of Sioux City, the sun is finally bright enough that I need sunglasses. An ambulance races by on the southbound side of the highway, lights flashing. Someone is in trouble somewhere.

∼

Route 121 east of Sioux Falls, South Dakota, is a narrow road, one lane each direction dividing fields of beans and corn, and it looks as much in the middle of nowhere as anywhere. I crest and then slide over gentle hills, past a white barn with a silo, an abandoned square red-brick building, cattle grazing. There's a water tower in the distance. Horses watch me pass from a fence line. A farmer on a green John Deere tractor drives down an access lane and into a field.

I'm nearly laughing, however. Everything I see makes me think of phrases like "grounded" or "down to earth," yet I'm driving to a place I've never been and hoping to talk about outer space. I have no idea what to expect. All I know is that there is a sign back on the interstate, a sign I've passed a thousand times, that reads "EROS Data Center," and one day I looked it up on the Web. Earth Resources Observation Systems. Satellites. Outer space, for some reason, in the southeastern corner of South Dakota.

A highway sign tells me this stretch of pavement has been adopted by the EROS Center Employee Association. Another sign, black with a green border on top, reads USGS and then EROS Data Center and points me down 252nd Street. I pass St. Paul's Cemetery and cruise over a hill, and suddenly, dramatically, there it is. A campus. A guard station. A wide, low blond-brick building. A satellite dish in front of the building's entrance. A smaller dish, pointed straight up, on the roof. A bubble, I think, encloses a third dish. The lawn is neatly cut, the grass baled, but the place is still a non sequitur.

At the front gate, the guard is armed. I stop and give him my name, and he checks me against a list on a clipboard. He radios to let the next guard, in the building, know I'm here, then tells me what door to drive to. In the parking lot there's a space reserved for the Make-a-Wish Foundation.

I'm told to enter a side door, where I meet another guard and surrender my driver's license. Then Dennis Hood appears in a Hawaiian shirt and a broad smile.

"You made it," he says.

"You're a saint," I say, "to wait so long on such a nice afternoon."

"Not a problem," he says. We shake hands and go inside.

A tour, he says, is the way to begin. And so we begin to walk the halls. Glass walls let me see into huge rooms with computers and monitors and racks of equipment I can't begin to understand. The main entry is set up like a museum. Display cases, models of satellites, historical legends explaining each exhibit. Photographs on the walls, as beautiful as any painting, show me the earth through the lens of a satellite, aimed by people who have questions about the natural world. Five hundred miles above the earth, ERTS-1, which was renamed Landsat-1, and then the many Landsats to follow have looked at vegetation, land use, mineral deposits, the way we use the things we need. There are greenness maps, pictures made by AVHRR, or Advanced Very High Resolution Radiometer. And there are the pictures from the NHAP, or National High Altitude Photography Program. There are satellite pictures of the Lewis and Clark route, complete with text from the journals, and there is the fact that these pictures, all of them, demand an emotional as well as an intellectual response.

After the tour, Dennis leads me to his office, where we sit and talk.

"I'm sitting here, in the middle of the prairie, with a guy in a Hawaiian shirt, talking about outer space," I say. "In many ways this is extraordinary. How did you wind up here?"

"It's perhaps a more direct path than you might imagine. I'm a Kansas kid, so I grew up on the prairie. Topeka and Lawrence. In any event, after I went into the Air Force and spent four years doing that, I got out and went back to school. Got a degree in geography."

"Where did you go to school?"

"University of Kansas. I had a nephew who had the temerity to go to Kansas State."

"I went to Mizzou," I say, bringing up the old rivalry between schools.

"That's OK," he says. "We tend to band together in this neck of the woods and resist the big red N."

"Anyway," I prompt, "a degree in geography and then?"

"I went to work for New York State Department of Transportation as a cartographer. They have a very active mapping program. But then my daughters got to be school age, and I didn't want to raise them in Albany, New York. I started casting about. I had an Air Force buddy who was, at the time, the revenue officer for the Department of Health in South Dakota. I asked if he knew of any job openings. He said, 'I'll call you back.' He did, and he said, 'There's an opening in the State Planning Office for something called a Land Use Planner. Are you one of those?' I said, 'I am now!' Wrote up a résumé; sent it off; got the job. About that same time, the Data Center was being built. I got in touch with the guy who was running the training program. He put on some training courses for the State Transportation Department, and he asked if I'd like to come to work for the Data Center, and I did."

"What year was that?" I ask.

"March of 1974."

"You've been here awhile, then."

"Yes."

"Always in pretty much the same capacity?"

"No. I've worked in every branch in the building except the computer branch. I'm not an IT person. In Training and Assistance we had a very active training program. I was in charge of the Land Use Unit. Once we had a big project working out in the Pacific Northwest, and I took a two-year temporary duty assignment out in Boise."

"What were you doing out there?"

"Coordinating a project that was transferring the applications of the technology to universities and state government in Oregon, Washington, and Idaho."

"Transferring the applications of the technology. What kinds of data?" I ask.

"Well, we would transfer raw or slightly processed Landsat data, geometrically corrected Landsat data, to the Idaho Department of Forestry or Water Resources. Their water people were very active, as you might imagine in a state with so much irrigated agriculture. It's a very, very powerful state agency. They, in fact, established a remote sensing unit that used satellite imagery and photography to depict land use and monitor conversion rates and that sort of thing. As you might expect, they're intensely interested in the amount of snowpack in the mountains. That enables them to predict how much water will be available for irrigation."

"From the launch pad to outer space, from orbit to EROS, from EROS to the tractor?" I ask.

"In a way, yes. Though not quite that direct."

"It's still impressive."

"You know," Dennis says, "I didn't say anything during our walk-around about our international activity. We have an extensive international program—funded largely by the U.S. Agency for International Development—USAID—here in the States. Primarily in the fields of food and famine warning, grazing capacity, and most of it concentrated in sub-Saharan Africa. The Sahel area. Although increasingly we're doing work in Central America with the coffee growers and others. It turns out to be a very, very useful tool. It sees vegetation very, very well. You asked about vegetation delineation earlier, how you separate alfalfa from corn. Yeah, you can. Pretty high degree of probability."

"That's based on something like a nitrogen reading?" I ask. "How would you from space tell the difference between soybeans and sugar beets?"

"Well, you fly over the area and acquire the imagery. You judge the vigor of the vegetation by the strength of its response in a particular portion of the electromagnetic spectrum. Then you compare that to a crop calendar that will typify a growing stage for a particular crop. Now, some of these things are given. You kind of know going in that Iowa will be heavy in corn. But if you're doing it in an area you don't know as well, you apply that kind of technology."

"When you're looking at Niger or the coffee stuff, what are they asking for, and what are you giving them?"

"It's interesting that you pick Niger," he says, "because the African headquarters for the technology that we've now transferred to them is in Niamey. But the way we started was with an appeal from USAID that said vegetation in this part of the world is an ephemeral condition. It comes on, the locusts eat it before the cattle get there, and the people starve. That's the cycle. There are extensive spraying programs, but that depends on keeping light planes or helicopters in the air: very expensive operation, very difficult to target the areas. They asked, 'Can you guys show us vegetation *as it is newly emerged* so that we can target our spraying activities and target our grazing activity?' We said, 'We think so, we think so.' We also work a lot with NOAA satellite data from an instrument called the Advanced Very High Resolution Radiometer, AVHRR. It's *not* very high resolution; it's kilometer resolution. Pretty gross look, but it's real good at spotting emerging vegetation. NOAA is very interested in the atmospherics and the clouds. They're not very interested in the ground flora, so we're at odds about scheduling spacecraft time immediately, and a limited amount of downlink time. So we built our own downlink for their data. It's a little birdbath-looking dealie, sits on the roof just about over our heads. If you look back when you drive out, you'll see it. It won't be tracking today, I don't think. If it's moving, it's tracking the satellite. So we can get their data, real time, turn it in a hurry, and make it available to managers on the ground to run their programs. For a period of time, before the technology was transferred to the African nations, we were diplomatic pouching data and analysis to Morocco on a biweekly basis that helped them assess grazing conditions. And the head of Morocco would quite literally get on his radio set for his fireside chat and tell his tribesmen where to move their cattle. So help me, it really did work that way for a while!"

Dennis has a fine laugh, I see.

"Now," I say, "I assume there's a computer room somewhere and it's just beamed over to them. They get it right there?"

"I'm not sure how they get it. We no longer have to pouch it over. It comes from the processing center immediately."

"Oh, so you're not even receiving the data. They are over there?"

"They get most of it directly over there. We do still supply some data. It's a terribly useful data set because you get so many looks so frequently. You may get seven or eight or ten looks a day. If you're looking at Landsat satellite imagery, you've got one pass over a given swath of earth. The next day's pass is immediately adjacent. The next day's pass is immediately adjacent to that, so it takes sixteen days to come back to the same point on the earth. If we're lucky and the cloud cover is just right and everything is OK and we get both Landsat 5 and Landsat 7, the best we can do with Landsat is look at something every eight days. There are advantages to multiple looks. Everything's a trade-off in this business. You can put a geostationary satellite in orbit and look at one spot on the earth pretty consistently day after day after day. If you want to look at the whole globe, you need a lot of them up there."

"What's the biggest picture you guys are receiving just in terms of square miles of coverage? Do you have one that's looking at all of the Northern Hemisphere?"

"No, 115 nautical miles on the side is our standard Landsat image. That's about the largest imagery we've got. It's a little hard to speak in absolutely discrete terms. There are some variabilities. Some of the satellites are slightly pointable. It changes the geometry a little bit and sees a little bit more of the surface. That's the standard feature."

"How many people did you say come through in a year?"

"About 15,000; 10,000 to 15,000."

"Lord, and you have to deal with all of them?"

"Oh, no. No, I don't. That includes scheduled guests. If we have a symposium and there are thirty-five professors here from around the globe, no, I don't meet them all. I have a very active and attentive seven-person staff. They do an awful lot of the outreach. We go to water festivals. We go to state fairs. We go to schools. We go to Kiwanis Clubs—most of that in the immediate geographic area. Some of it farther-flung. There's a conference out in San Diego later this month put on by a software company called ESRL. We'll have two Outreach people there—staffing a booth that is a U.S. Geological Survey booth. We'll have an EROS Data Center portion of that. We try to get around mostly to professional meetings and symposia."

"Seven-person staff working for you. How many people are employed by the Center all together?"

"On-site, about six hundred. Off-site about another sixty or seventy."

"What do the off-site people do?"

"The same things we do, only in other places. I pointed out the mission operations control center down the hall. There's a replica of that at Goddard Space Flight Center in Greenbelt, Maryland. We staff that one as well. We talk to one another and back one another up. It's a fail-safe operation. NASA still flies the bird. They have the responsibility for the satellite platform. We control the sensor and the acquisitions and the programming."

"OK, so they don't act as an intermediary for any command on that level for you on the satellite?"

"Right. There's no approval. They keep it in orbit. They keep it accurately pointed, at the right pitch, tilt, and yaw. We acquire the data. This organization is unique among U.S. Geological Survey organizations, and most government agencies, in that only sixty of those, well, seventy now, of those six hundred on-sites are federal employees. All the rest are contract employees. The current primary contractor is an outfit called SAIC—Space Applications International Corporation."

"They are a technology firm? What is their part of this?"

"They are a high-tech firm. They're a heavy-duty contractor like Boeing and Ratheon and others. That's the bulk of their business—high-tech engineering."

"But what they're doing here is maintaining the equipment, receiving and interpreting data, what?"

"Everything from clerical secretarial to PhD geophysicist. Quite a span of technical knowledge. Most of it's pretty high-tech—advanced degrees, specialization in one field or another. It might be something as general as forestry or as specific as how to design and build various sensors."

"Who sets the future agenda for what's needed in earth imaging satellites? Do you guys go down to NASA and say this is what we need in twenty years, and please build us a satellite, or do you just get whatever they decide what somebody else wants?"

"That's a very good question. The answer could be longish, but the short take on it is that all of that really happens with an awful lot of cross talk and consultation. NASA supports a fairly vast retinue of principal investigators that are looking at the applications of the data or looking at different sensor designs."

Dennis pauses.

"Everybody wants the same information, just in a different shade, eh?" I ask. Behind him, through the window, I can see birds whirling in the now clear blue sky. "Tell me a story," I say. "I mean, everybody looked at the swelling of the side of Mount Saint Helens. We should have seen it. In retrospect, it was so obvious. It's embarrassing nobody said the time was right now. Then again, there's all the Chicken Little stories too. We were talking yesterday about the guy who predicted the New Madrid fault would go again. This was ten years ago because of whatever planetary alignment sets up the super high tides. It was measuring the ground stress. He said these two combined—it's going to go. USGS came out and said, no it's not. He's running the equivalent of a vegetable stand now. The potential for embarrassment is there too. So tell me a story. One that you missed or one that you got."

"The USGS is such a conservative organization that, as you discovered talking to your earthquake man, they're pretty reluctant to go very far out on a limb. We did manage to get our wrists slapped by responding too quickly, once upon a time. It happened that the Landsat satellite was crossing over Chernobyl just about the time that things began to literally heat up over there. Of course, there's a . . . "

"This was coincidence. It wasn't . . . I mean, Landsat is not an intelligence satellite."

"No, and you can't steer it very much except to kind of keep it in or-bit. You don't shift the orbital path easily. So it really was serendipitous. It happened to be there at the time. We got an image that indicated serious heat buildup in a couple of reactors and cooling ponds that cool the reactors. We thought, what a great opportunity to go public and show off a little bit. And so we turned that image over to the local news people at the same time we sent it back to our headquarters and let them pursue whatever release they chose to back there. Well, the next day, we had a call from the Department of State saying, "*We* will be the spokesperson for international incidents. Thank you very much. Please let us know when this happens again."

"Would that have been a human eye scanning an image? Or would that have been a computer saying, Here's the change?"

"Well, first, there were rumors and curiosity about . . . Someone else had pointed out that there was unusual activity there. It happened that the satellite was going over."

"By someone else, you mean a different department, a different . . . or was there somebody here?"

"No, someone external to here. I really don't know who. It was kind of in the news, that there was a buzz about something happening. So we acquired an image, and it turned out to be fairly revealing because, at the time, the Soviets were saying there was one reactor in trouble, and it was pretty clear that three of them were. So we said that and got told not to say it again!"

Dennis's laugh is deep and genuine.

"Nonetheless, you probably did, from the public side, a great service to get that image out there as fast as possible?"

"I hope so. I hope it's viewed that way. Again, none of our imagery is classified. It's of a resolution that's coarse enough so that it's really not useful strategically. We tend to do the before and after thing pretty well."

"Why the armed guard for the site then? Is it just the expensiveness of the equipment?"

"$50 million worth of computers and a fragile data set."

"Backed up somewhere."

"No sir."

"So, if a building burns and it's all gone?"

"If the building is destroyed, it would largely be gone. Now, there are foreign ground stations that have their own collections in archives. And we have worked pretty hard to provide digital archive backup for some of the more recent data. It's not perfect and it's not in place. It certainly doesn't cover historical data. We are at risk."

"Tell me a success story?"

"The stories in the Sahel I think are compelling and pretty successful. Hopefully, we provide data that let land managers and administrators and decision makers have a little bit better way to make their decisions. We provide a variety of vegetation-related inputs to the interagency fire centers in Boise and in Missoula."

"Can you do a radar moisture-content imaging? Can you tell how dry a forest is?"

"No, not really. There's a fair amount of work being done with soil moisture, but again, we don't penetrate very far . . . It's a little tough to do. But if we have historical imagery that shows us what the forest looked like last year or the brush land looked like last year, we can develop an index that gives you the relative vigor and amount of vegetation present. It dies off in the fall. Next summer, it's not vegetation—it's fire fuel."

"I would imagine you're doing work like looking at the Yellowstone fire now. Seeing how robust is the recovery? Where is it strongest? That kind of stuff."

"Yellowstone, California, Alaska. Got an image the other day. We're doing quarterly reporting and a scientist showed a new MODIS image of Alaska that shows—what did I say—fifty-some fires burning in that area?"

"Sixty-eight-plus fires is your note on the side."

"All the squiggles are fires. That's a big guy," he says, placing his finger on the image, "but there are lots of little ones."

"This is where I'm going. If you want to be really jealous of my trip, my friend in Fairbanks is a pilot. He's going to take me out. He's got what's called a Widgeon, which is . . . "

"A great airplane!"

"Well, we're going to get in his Widgeon one morning. We're going to fly out to some small little lake and annoy some trout."

"Good for you!"

Dennis and I walk outside, past a display case for softball trophies and Soap Box Derby awards, talking about motorcycles. He tells me my trip has a name among motorcycle riders—the Ironbutt. I tell him I'll be in touch, that I hope to finish the route if the news from my father doesn't turn me around. We shake hands, and the last image I have of Dennis is a man in a Hawaiian shirt, on a motorcycle, receding into the distance on a county road, framed by a government installation and satellite dishes on one side and cornfields on the other.

~

7:35 p.m. I-29 north. The sun is setting to the west. A coyote roams the edge of a crop field on the eastern side of the highway. No clouds to speak of. Bright blue sky, no haze, cool temperature. It's only 70 degrees. If there's humidity, I can't feel it. Hay bales stand in their fields. It's a calendar picture of middle America in the middle of the summer. I can't help but be amazed at the work being done not so very far behind me now. To look and to listen and to feel the earth underneath us and try to make sense of it all. To send the cameras of all sorts into space to get a better picture of where we are and what we're doing. It has nothing to do with who's running the show, whether a Republican or a Democrat is president. It has everything to do with understanding and caring for the planet we live on. For miles in front of me, the rest of South Dakota and then North Dakota and the short jog over to Minnesota are familiar miles. I've driven them a hundred times or more. And yet every day the light is different, the green is different, the clouds are different. Every day, I'm different. It is an extraordinary drive no matter how many times. Fargo is 218 miles in front of me.

9:48 p.m.—I-29 north in South Dakota. I cross the continental divide into a basis of water that now flows north, eventually into the Red River and into Lake Winnipeg and into Hudson Bay—one of the remaining vestiges of glacial Lake Agassiz.

I'm listening to a nationwide oldies show on the radio, people calling in from all over the country. A couple named Joe and Kim call in. They're doing Route 66. Nowhere to go and all day to get there, Joe says. They're just doing the road because the road is there. They want to hear some Stones, so the DJ plays them *Satisfaction*.

Eleven o'clock at night—a quarter moon hangs in the sky. There are stars in the clear summertime sky. I cross the Red River into Minnesota, and will soon be home to the arms of my children and then my wife.

Day Four

Day four begins at six o'clock in the morning. I-94 west exits onto I-29 north as the Jeep and I light out for the territory at seventy miles an hour. The Jeep leans into the long, sweeping exit, and I feel the centrifugal force push me to the door, feel the edge between the arc the Jeep is tracing and the speed we're keeping, I suddenly wonder how much more it would take to really fly, to launch myself and my Jeep into some other expectation. I know rockets need a certain amount of thrust, need a certain velocity to break the insistent pull back home. Yet I also remember reading somewhere, though I don't remember where, that a rocket in orbit is really falling toward earth the whole time—but the curve of the earth means the planet keeps getting out of the way of the fall. We merge into the northbound traffic and climb a small hill by the shopping mall. I press on the gas.

Clear sky with a few wispy cirrus clouds and an orange sun rising in the east.

This is the day that will take me across the border, up into Winnipeg, up into Canada, then left and west on the Trans-Canada Highway, then the west on the Yellowhead Highway. This will be a long day, maybe nineteen hours behind the wheel to get to Edmonton, Alberta, tonight. Longer than I normally like to drive. But news may come about my father's surgery date. If I'm going to make it to the Arctic coast, I'll have to get there fast.

On the phone with my father last night, I asked how he was feeling, if there was any news. He asked, "What news are you expecting? There won't be any news until tomorrow, and maybe not even then. And the only news will be what day I go in for the operation." Clear enough, I think.

Up to seventy miles an hour, and then quickly back down to thirty-five as I pass through construction zones. A billboard, one of those put up by the billboard company when no other ad is there, black letters on a white background, simply says "Have a Great Day."

When I have told people that the land here is flat, they have nodded as if they understood. Flat, in their experience of the earth, means mostly flat, or nearly flat. There's a dale in the distance, or a hollow, a meadow that slopes toward some creek. If you drop a marble, it rolls away. When they visit here, however, they look almost startled. This is flat, they say. Completely flat. Horizon to horizon, not even a bump. It's both disturbing and magnificent.

This is, I tell people, the bed of old Lake Agassiz. 11,500 years ago, this bit of flatland prairie was underwater. It was under the water of the largest freshwater lake the planet has ever seen. The Laurentide ice sheet, which once covered nearly all of Canada east of the Rocky Mountains and was heavy enough to press the earth down nearly a kilometer, was already shrinking, retreating under the skies of the warming planet. Once big enough, with spurs into Iowa and Illinois, the glacier's meltwater had run down the Mississippi. But a line had been crossed. A continental divide had been formed, one side flowing south to the Gulf, one side flowing north. Today the Red River flows north, into Lake Winnipeg, then finally into Hudson Bay. But back then the ice itself prevented the meltwater from escaping, so it pooled, and pooled, and the lake rose flush against the ice.

There are beaches in North Dakota and Minnesota, not thirty miles from where I live. Hills where the water once lapped. Once, when the lake found a new outlet and the water level fell one hundred meters almost instantly, the water ran down the St. Lawrence River and into the North Atlantic—so much cold freshwater all at once, the scientists say, that the ocean's transfer of heat from the tropics to the Arctic was confused and halted. The whole planet cooled, the ice formed again, that outlet was sealed, and the whole thing started over. When the melting began again, the outlet followed the Mackenzie River and emptied into the Arctic Ocean.

In the Pleistocene, on the shores of Lake Agassiz, there were mammoths and dire wolves and North American camels. And close behind them, hunting, came humans. Today, just the Red River and the endless fields of sugar beets and grain. Flat ground. Already I pass license plates for Washington State and Saskatchewan, one from Manitoba. Windsocks on buildings show me the wind is from the south this morning, which is a good sign—an omen. Wind that pushes the Jeep increases the gas mileage substantially. Wind that pushes against the Jeep makes for an expensive ride. On the radio, I learn that this is the day Eisenhower signed the truce ending the Korean War. I hear that President Bush is enjoying reading the 9/11 Commission report. He says it reads like a mystery novel, and I am bothered deeply by the disconnect.

As the highway parallels Hector International Airport, I see a soccer complex to the east. Fields of grains, fields of beans. Round bales stacked together neatly. Late July on the prairie. Full-time harvest is not so far away. Right now, barring storms, the farmers know what they've got. A red-tailed hawk perches on a fence post. The sky gets brighter every second. If you believe in things like possibility, I think, morning on the prairie is a good time to see it.

On National Public Radio's morning show, a little Oscar Peterson before the news, then some bluegrass music. A tune called "Let 'Em Run." Another billboard with black letters on a white background, a simpler message: "Be Polite." A pocket gopher darts east across the highway. A red-winged blackbird crosses the highway going west. As I approach a bridge, what seems like a thousand barn swallows descend from the beams and dance around the opening. A red stain on the highway in the passing lane is smeared fifty yards, ending at the road-killed deer left by the roadside.

7:30 in the morning, somewhere north of Grand Forks, North Dakota, the fields are already harvested, the soil turned once again to black. Clouds building to the west. The radio tells me there may be storms and showers later this afternoon. Other fields still stand tall, waiting for the combine or the harvester. The town of Drayton arrives, and a sign on the interstate announces that Drayton is the catfish capital of the world. At the Pembina exit, another black-and-white billboard. This one reads, "Do Your Best."

And then the Canadian border.

~

8:39 in the morning and I hand my passport to the Customs officer at the drive-up window.

"You've been through here before," he says.

"Many times," I reply.

He asks me the usual questions. Where am I going? How long will I be in the country? What is the purpose of my trip? How much money am I bringing? Do I have any weapons? Perhaps I anticipate the questions and answer them a bit too quickly, because the officer asks me to park the Jeep and go inside. He doesn't say why.

The inside of the Customs office has the charm of a drivers' license office. Tile floor, fluorescent lights, uncomfortable chairs. Little windows at a counter, like a teller's window at a bank, where you have to explain yourself, your hope to enter the country, your excuse for some transgression. There is already a family at the one open window, and a biker already waiting, sitting in one of the chairs, so I find a chair for myself, and wait. It's impossible not to hear the conversation at the window.

The family at the window is being turned away from Canada. He is a citizen of Paraguay. She is a citizen of the Philippines. Somewhere in their late thirties, early forties, they have two children, a boy and a girl, playing at their feet. Living and working in the United States, they have applied but not been classified as permanent residents. Citizens and permanent residents of the United States do not need a visa to enter Canada. Citizens of Paraguay and the Philippines apparently do. The man and the woman plead while their children tug on them, laugh, have no idea what's going on. The man makes a phone call to relatives or friends and says, "We have to turn back. 750 miles!" This is not a happy morning for them. When they leave, the gray-haired biker in leather jacket and chaps, although not a mean-looking sort, has to explain why he's got a pistol-grip shotgun with him. You can disassemble it, he tries to explain. He's on his way to Alaska too. Customs isn't mean to the man, but it's not accommodating either. Eventually he's allowed to proceed.

When it is my turn, the woman who helps me at the desk says she just wants to make sure. But I don't know what she was trying to make sure of. Do I have enough money? How long am I going be in the country? Am I bringing anything I plan to leave? The same questions I was asked outside. She's very pleasant, though. When I tell her I'm going to make Edmonton tonight, she says, "That's industrious." Then, "Wait. Industrious isn't the right word. What word am I looking for?"

"Silly?" I offer.

"No."

"Foolish?"

"No. Ambitious!"

She thumbs through the pages of my passport, looking at the designs of other stamps and visas, and then I'm sent on my way. On my way out, I notice one detail. The Customs officers are all wearing flak jackets, bulletproof vests. The men and women of the cleaning crew working around them are not.

A mile or two up the road, I stop at the Manitoba Visitors and Welcome Center. Bright paint, flags snapping in the wind, the building looks cheerful and prosperous even under the gunmetal sky. I exchange a little bit of money, fill my coffee cup, and talk with the two women who work the information counter and currency exchange. They say they are glad for the company. I say I'm already glad to stretch my legs. When they ask where I'm going and I tell them Edmonton still tonight, they say, "Wow, you've still got fourteen hours of driving in front of you." My guess is they don't think I'll make it.

Back on the highway now, I pass a sign that says, "Welcome to the Pembina Valley. Spread Your Wings." The speed limit is posted in kilometers. Green fields stretch away from both sides of the highway. Power lines to the west, a railway on the east. Wind still from the south, clouds still building to the west. It's a beautiful day in Manitoba. In the bed of old Lake Agassiz, the land is as flat as is ever possible. The town of St. Jean Baptiste. The "Soup Pea Capital of the World." Bright yellow fields of canola.

I pass a sign for the Red River Floods Interpretive Site and feel an urge to stop, though I press on the gas. The 1997 Red River Flood is a valley story. It starts with more than one hundred inches of snowfall in an area that normally gets thirty in a winter. It starts with the shape of the Red River Valley, the fact that the river flows north. In springtime, the south end of the river thaws first, but then tries to flow north against the still hard ice. Just like Lake Agassiz. In 1997 there were seven official blizzards. A friend of mine, a meteorologist, says there really were eight blizzards, but one of them isn't counted because no one issued a blizzard warning. Every blizzard brought snow and wind and ice, and every blizzard found us all digging out. One or two days after New Year's, my wife and kids and I were trying to drive back home from visiting my parents in Missouri. Normally it's a ten-hour drive with stops to eat. In 1997 it took us three days. Just north of a gas stop in Sioux City, Iowa, we drove into the heart of one of the storms. No visible road. No visible distance. The storm seemed to sit on us, hard. We drove by the reflected light of the tenth-of-a-mile markers and somehow, slowly, eventually found first a gas station at the Vermillion, South Dakota exit, and then the last hotel room in town. Trapped by snow, halted by highway closings. But safe, and warm.

More than one hundred inches of snow—heavy snow, laden snow—and the flatland prairie to drain it. Flood stage for the Red River in Fargo and Moorhead is seventeen feet. The river rose to more than thirty feet. My wife and I filled and stacked and placed sandbags at the homes of friends, at the homes of colleagues and neighbors, at the homes of people we didn't know at all. The river continued to rise. The foundation of our house at the time is made of cinder blocks, and there was so much water in the ground, and so much pressure behind that water, the cracks between the blocks became springs, water shooting out from the walls in a hundred places. Our basement drain plugged against the advent of backup, we hauled water from our basement to dump in the backyard, only to haul it out again five minutes later.

A good bit of Fargo went underwater. Towns like Dilworth and Ada, Minnesota, neither one on the banks of the river, went underwater from the overland flooding. Grand Forks went underwater, and then caught on fire as well. The flood crossed the border and then went around the dike protecting the town of Ste. Agathe. The CBC described it in military language as the first town to fall. People left by car and then were evacuated by any means possible. On television, we watched families leaving in the buckets of front-end loaders, then in canoes and fishing boats.

Then Winnipeg. After a flood in 1950, Winnipeg dug a forty-seven-kilometer floodway called Duff's Ditch to divert floodwater around the town. And in 1997, it worked.

So many stories stacked up on any place! Laurentide. Agassiz. Tyrannosaurus. Mastodon. Sioux. Cree. Viking. Yankee. Voyageur. Even Winnie-the-Pooh, as the character was named after a Canadian black bear called Winnipeg at a London zoo. I have been here before, and these are stories I know. But when I come upon a sign for the Riel Industrial Park, I am, again, amazed at how a border can stop a story, how a line on a map can keep a history contained. Louis Riel, born in Manitoba in 1844, tried to be a priest and then tried to be a lawyer, but instead he became what has been called the father of Manitoba, and the most controversial person in Canadian history. Riel became the leader of the Métis people of the Red River Valley. The Métis, the children of French fur traders or Hudson's Bay Company employees and Cree, Ojibway, or Saulteaux women, quickly became a group, a people. United against the Hudson's Bay Company and the government of Canada, they fought for basic rights. There was no Manitoba then. This earth, this road where this morning I watch red-winged blackbirds play in the grasses just off the pavement, was in the huge, vague, promising, and frightening Northwest Territories. In 1869, Riel led the Red River Rebellion. Establishing a provisional government, Riel and the Métis negotiated with the Canadian government and worked to create a province called Assiniboia. Their work became the Manitoba Act, and Manitoba joined the confederation of Canadian provinces. But the Métis had arrested, tried, and executed a man named Thomas Scott, a pro-Canadian. After the act had been passed and the federal troops showed up to become the law, people in Ontario wanted Riel to pay. He fled to Montana and was then elected three times to the Canadian parliament, though he was never able to take his seat. The Métis moved west, into Saskatchewan, and again there were problems and grievances. The leaders wanted Riel to return, to bring their issues to the federal government, and sent a party to collect him. He did return. But the world turned badly and the battle of Duck Lake was followed by the battle of Fish Lake, which was followed by the battle of Batoche and the battle of Loon Lake. The North-West Rebellion failed. Riel was captured, tried by a jury that found him guilty of treason but suggested mercy, and then sentenced to death by the judge. This trial, often called the most famous one in Canadian history, and still a sore point between French Canadians and English Canadians, is not even a whisper south of the border. No history class looks north. No elementary school classroom speaks the word Métis or Riel. A shame. Perhaps even a sin. History and culture are always local, always bound to particular people, real people, and real events. The Red River Valley is where I live. Its stories are my stories. Each one should be told, and told loudly, on both sides of the border.

~

10:09 in the morning and I'm on the west side of Winnipeg, on the perimeter highway, skirting the city to make some fast time west. Storm clouds come together and form a dark shape to the west of me. I'll be driving into rain soon. The dark clouds set right over the bright yellow canola fields, and then sunshine from the east fills the picture, reflects gold from the crops to the sky. On a notepad resting on the passenger seat, I write the words *storm, fat light, huge,* and *thrilling.*

I pass a marker for the Principal Meridian. This is the boundary line, the surveyor's line, that began the ordering of the new territory: 97°27.5' west of Greenwich. This line, and what it represented, started the rebellions as much as Riel or anyone else. Townships from here to the Rocky Mountains. Order. Control. More rain comes, but it isn't very hard and doesn't last long. The highway is dry, clear, and fast.

It would be easy to look out over these fields—these fields that seem larger than the fields of North Dakota because of the lack of fences, the lack of borders—and it would be easy to say that this is a place where nothing happens. No skyscrapers. No airports. No fancy restaurants. No intrigue. No theater. Just an endless view of summer crops growing well. But that is perhaps the great deception of the prairie. What happens here is gargantuan, huge. From the sky, tornadoes, hail, blizzards, lethal sunshine. From the earth, enough food to feed the world. From the people, few celebrities. Just work that matters. On the prairie, scale is everything. And the scale is big.

The town of Portage la Prairie comes and goes, and then Route 16, the Yellowhead, diverges from Route 1. The Yellowhead route across Canada is called the new Trans-Canada Highway on billboards and on maps. Although I won't see it, Riding Mountain National Park is 166 kilometers in front of me. I've never been there. But there are stories we carry, gifts from friends, images of bliss or hell we pack as forecast or warning. Riding Mountain is where Jim and Eleanor Coomber, two good friends, spent their honeymoon. After a college dinner one night, all of us mingling and delaying our exit, I mentioned this to two other friends, Dick and Tracey Moorhead, only to discover they had spent their honeymoon in the same place. The two couples had known each other for decades. But this was a new story between them. I remember the broad, honest smiles on their faces, and I am saddened that my Jeep will not turn that way.

11:43 in the morning and scanning the radio I come upon a French-language station. I don't speak a word of French, but I immensely enjoy listening to it this morning. My son, this whole week, is living at a French immersion camp.

~

11:54 in the morning and I pass a sign that says that in 1857 I would now have been entering the Northwest Territories. I can see hills in the northern distance. Yellow fields of canola still surround the highway. This whole corridor is filled with U-pick strawberries. I pass the Arden Ridge, the main beach of Lake Agassiz. Then I come to Neepawa. The town sign says, "If you can't stop, smile as you drive through. Population: 996,600 short of one million."

Outside the Esso station in Neepawa, a sign says "Welcome to Club Happy." A man in a tie runs out to pump my gas for me. He greets me happily. "How're you doing?" I'd swear the man is beaming.

I'm slow to unfold myself out of the Jeep, back and leg muscles unwilling to flex and bend again. "Sat too long already, eh?" the man asks.

Inside, the desk clerk, late high school maybe college age, greets me with a "How're you doing, sir?" "Fine," I say.

When they are done filling the Jeep, there's a problem with my credit card. The card isn't declined or over the limit—it's just from the States. Their computer doesn't recognize it. They are filled with apologies as they dig out a manual and read the instructions for authorizing my sale. Each new customer is greeted with enthusiasm and apologies for the delay. Every customer responds with glee. It's more than a little scary. The men and women who come in and out of the station are the politest people I've ever seen. Everything is a "please." Everything is a "thank you." People hold doors for each other. I linger by the magazine rack just to listen. When I go back out to the Jeep, the young man who originally tried to run my card is pumping gas. "You have a good day, sir," he yells. I assure him I will. When he was running my card, the manager, wearing a tie, said he'd have to call in for authorization. I told him that was fine with me. He said, "But I won't do it now." He said, "I'll do that later when things aren't so busy." "What if the card's declined?" I ask. "Ah," he says. "I trust you."

12:39 in the afternoon. The Yellowhead makes a short right-hand turn, and suddenly the road heads into hills. Forests have been cleared in some areas. I cross the Little Saskatchewan River. On the radio, a CBC show asks the question, Should the government forbid churches to offer sanctuary to those seeking refugee status? Does that provide a backdoor to the immigration system? Nearly everyone seems to think the system should be preserved.

I pass the biker with the pistol-grip shotgun. Pulled over on the side of the road and rooting around in one of his saddlebags, he's on his way to Alaska too.

～

2:04 in the afternoon and I'm driving on the side of the first valley that deserves the name. Broad and green, a purple-flowered crop paints the sides. The Assiniboine River runs at the bottom. Far western Manitoba. Farmland from here to every horizon.

2:08 in the afternoon and I cross into Saskatchewan. Yellow fields of canola. Blue sky now, cotton-ball clouds. In Langenburg, near the roadway, is the world's largest swing—the two-seat kind that you pump back and forth facing each other. It's called the Goliath. Very tall, red metal, from a distance it looks like an oil rig, or maybe a tepee. No one rides it now, but I can imagine the carloads of children rising out of the stupor of backseat wars on summer road trips and demanding to swing on the world's largest swing, to have their time with Goliath. And I admit there is a part of me that remembers much smaller, backyard versions of this swing, standing on the back of the seat and holding on to the bars and pumping with all my weight and might to get that swing to fly. I remember riding the back of the seat on the upswing at turning, twisting at the apex to try and launch myself into the air. There is a part of me that would like to stop here and play, but there are too many miles still to go today. I press on the gas.

West of town, the miles and kilometers go easy. Open space, open sky. No real traffic, and the few cars that whisk by me heading east seem like friends. Their drivers smile, raise a few fingers off the steering wheel in a small wave, which I return. It's entirely possible to forget there is any such thing as destination. This, I think. This moment, this movement, seems complete. And then, because this is the prairie in summertime, because this is a place where the mind can wander and range, I find myself thinking about Einstein. The speed and position of an object is relative to the speed and position of the observer. My speed is 110 kilo-

156

meters an hour. My position is the driver's seat of a Jeep, heading west toward mountains and, with luck, adventure. I know the world would look very different if I were to stop, if I were to examine even one small roadside weed as a particular thing, if I were to investigate one idiosyncratic person's story. But from this speed, and from this position, the prairie is both history and potential unending. I have no idea how far outside Princeton Einstein got when he was in America, but it's a pleasant fantasy to imagine him here this day.

It's tough to use the word "suddenly" here. You can see forever. If something is a threat, it's visible a long time before it's a danger. Sure, things can spring up from the roadside. In general, though, this a place where anticipation is a source of comfort instead of worry. In the mountains every bend, every valley, every cliff face has its own immediate presence and the mind is focused on what is immediate. Here, the immediate is a range of hundreds of square miles. Would it be fair to say the prairie is the most imaginable or imaginative space on the planet? Radio off, I find myself dreaming memories of being here before, of being in the outback of Australia, or being in a desert, of being in the glare of tremendous ice fields, in other open spaces. It sounds forced, I know. But on the prairie it's possible, it's easy, to bring the whole planet close.

I ride for hours with the radio off. Then I turn the radio on and enjoy the full, uninterrupted length of a symphony. I know tomorrow I'll be held by the spectacle of mountains, or by the gravity of earth rising up in front of me. So unlike where I live, it will demand every bit of attention I have. I will give it not only happily but gleefully, even giggly at times. Here in Saskatchewan, however, where the planet looks very much like the planet I know back home, it's possible to dream the larger questions.

Coming into the town of Yorkton, signs tell me I can buy a Bowflex or a Boston pizza. Canadian television and the Royal Canadian Mounted Police are at a cemetery on the outskirts of town, either because there's trouble or for a memorial. I don't know.

~

Sometimes it's easy to make connections. Some days it seems as if every person, every building, every field, and every river somehow sparks a memory, a story, some part of personal history that says, *me too*. And some days it's easy to feel like a foreigner, completely estranged and divorced from that day's touch. But more often than not, it's the connections that press against the experience.

3:13 in the afternoon and I pass a big Chevy truck pulling a chrome Airstream trailer. The license plate reads Ohio. Like me, they're heading west toward Alaska.

3:32 in the afternoon and I come upon the town of Insinger and an onion-dome church. I don't see a sign out front. It's brown, wooden, clearly Ukrainian. Greek Orthodox, I think. I have never been inside an Orthodox church, though I've paused over pictures in coffee-table books. If I were to stop, to pull up to that church, to pull or push on the front door and enter, what would I find? Anyone? Anything at all? History? Hope?

3:43 in the afternoon and I'm at the Quill Lakes International Bird Area. A broad, shimmering lake bordered by mudflats and low hills. No boat or canoe breaks the water. Beautiful and quiet in the afternoon light. Here, I think! Here is fine work. This is a place I have heard of before. Quill Lakes is part of the Western Hemisphere Shorebird Reserve Network. Sixty sites in eight countries, from Alaska to the end of Patagonia, land given over to the health and preservation of shorebirds. A part of the migratory bird flyways, these places and their owners give themselves to the movement of birds. I have a note that lists the birds seen here: American avocet, Baird's sandpiper, black-bellied plover, buff-breasted sandpiper, common snipe, dunlin, greater yellowlegs, Hudsonian godwit, killdeer, least sandpiper, long-billed dowitcher, marbled godwit, pectoral sandpiper, red knot, red phalarope, ruddy turnstone, sanderling, semipalmated plover, semipalmated sandpiper, short-billed dowitcher, stilt sandpiper, western sandpiper, whimbrel, willet.

I smile as I remember the killdeer that nested at the base of a tree in my backyard two summers ago. Every time we approached, the adult bird would limp away from the nest, feigning a broken wing, trying to lure me toward what must surely be an easier target. And when I was far enough away from the nest and too close to the bird, it would transform into a vision of health as it took to the air and flew away. I have no proof, of course. But I like to think that bird, its mate, and then its chicks spent time here, near this lake. I like to think this space and my space are connected that way.

Then, near the town of Leslie, I have no idea what I'm looking at. A cleared field with fifty, maybe sixty, round tents. Like yurts from Mongolia, but these look like plastic. And they are not big enough for people. Some of them are light blue. Others are orange. White roofs. Each of them maybe fifty yards from the other. The fields here are huge, so these shelters give the impression of an encampment. Some odd army, or perhaps the gypsies. Boy Scouts or a church group. But I don't see any people. My next thought is dog houses. But there are no dogs. Then I think bird shelters, though I've never seen any like these, and I don't see any birds, not even one, waddling around the igloo style openings. On the notepad in the Jeep I write, "Find out about the bird shelters." And though I have no way of knowing this now, several months from now, back in my study at home, when I come to this page, and see this sentence again, I will pause, then spend half an hour looking for what kind of bird would live in this kind of shelter. Giving up, I will call the Foam Lake RCMP, and then the Saskatchewan crop insurance department. I'll send an e-mail to a man named Jim McDougall, whose name is at the bottom of the city Web sites I explore looking for the answer. When he replies, he says,

> I am assuming you are referring to the round orange and blue tent like structures in a field on the north side of the highway just east of Leslie. These are bee shelters, empty for the winter but left in the field. The bees are kept in a warm building over winter. Leaving the shelters out this year was not a good idea, we had a very strong wind last month and many of the shelters are damaged. Some have been torn to shreds, some were blown away and found in the trees. I don't know who owns these bees and shelters but if you want to know more, I can inquire and let you know.

Amazing, I think. These are not bird shelters at all. They're! Leafcutter bees, to pollinate the alfalfa crops. I learn from the insurance department that alfalfa producers must keep 20,000 bees per acre. But back on the road, looking right at them, what I imagine is yurts.

4:30 in the afternoon and the exit for the town of Mozart, Saskatchewan. Gas is fifteen kilometers in front of me and the needle is bouncing on E.

4:33 and I pass Harvard Road.

5:04 in the afternoon, after leaving the town of Wynyard, the Foam Lake Heritage Marsh appears on the right. Another part of the network for birds, another broad vision reflecting the summer sky. Beautiful, and quiet. A low-power, in-town radio station tells me there are 5,000 acres to this marsh. The radio station tells me where the lookouts are, the self-guided tours, the hiking trails. More orange yurts, then a sign for Ducks Unlimited, Canada. The radio calls this the "gem of the prairie marshes." Another field of yurts, only this time powder blue.

$\sim$

Afternoon turns toward evening. The radio spins through stations without catching a signal, then locks on a loud country station. I turn the radio off. The showers I've been dodging all day find the roadway again. I drive through rain, then not, then rain again. Still an hour in front of me, the city of Saskatoon. After that, more prairie on the road to Edmonton. At six o'clock, an extra layer of cumulus clouds forms beneath the usual one. Long and fat, they move like a flotilla of schooners just about the ground. Rain falls from those on the south side of the highway.

A license plate from Nova Scotia.

The clouds part, the sun shines. I arrive in the town of Saskatoon. Suddenly the Yellowhead feels like an expressway again. Off ramps and on ramps, chain-link fence at the end of the right-of-way, a separation between the highway and the yards of homes and apartments. There are streetlights and exit signs. There are high-rise apartment buildings. There is an exit for College Drive.

I'd be hard-pressed to say this is a traffic jam; but it's certainly more traffic than I've encountered for the past six or seven hours. My attention now is on the roadway—the traffic, the press of people in cars and trucks around me. I'm taken aback when I look up and see a small hill I hadn't noticed beyond the buildings and traffic, then a bridge over the South Saskatchewan River. Beautiful, wide, and apparently shallow, the river cuts through town. There are paths on the banks, buildings that look to the water. I try to slow, to look at the water, but the bridge takes me off the other end too fast, and my focus is on the guy driving the U-Haul truck in front of me.

Bring a lot of people together and you can call it a city. You get wonderful things: the arts, business. And you get terrible things: poverty and crime. But what you get, no matter what, whether it's wonderful or terrible, is a focus on the self. On people. Hills are no longer important, except as something to be managed. Turning left off the Yellowhead to find a gas station, what bothers me is how much this place looks like every place else. Same design. Same needs. Tough to tell you whether I'm here or anywhere else like here.

At the Esso in Saskatoon, an attendant named Aaron doesn't quite know how to handle my credit card. A paper sale, he has to call for authorization. He calls and gets authorization. But then he calls his manager. The manager says to go for it. Then he sits. Every *i* is dotted and every *t* is crossed. He figures out the number of liters, and then I make the mistake of trying to buy a cup of coffee. The coffee is sold out. He has to make another pot. He rummages for filters and then for the ground beans. I ask him to put the coffee on the gas ticket, but he doesn't know how to write that on the receipt that had been authorized for the amount of the gas purchase. I pay him cash for the coffee. Almost thirty minutes to buy a little more than a quarter tank of gas and a cup of coffee before I leave Saskatoon.

On the west side of Saskatoon the Yellowhead is a series of stoplights, then an exit back onto the freeway. Then suddenly the city ends. The prairie returns. The speed limit is 110 kilometers an hour. Flatland, big sky, CBC radio still within range. The wind comes up hard and strong from the west, pressing against the Jeep. I can feel the engine strain as it hasn't all day. Ahead of me, now that I'm out of Saskatoon, it seems the clouds are closing in again. Rain cells forming in front of me.

～

Sometimes you wish for direct line to *National Geographic* or somebody else who publishes the pictures that make you stop, that make you aware of your own heart and lungs, that somehow move the speed of time. A small rise west of Saskatoon and suddenly what I see, uninterrupted in the western distance, is a thunderhead. The whole thing. Dark and ominous at the base, soft-focus white fluff at the top. It's a hard contrast against the sky, the yellow canola fields, the green other fields. In the sunshine, I can see dark rain falling from below. This is the calendar shot, I think. The one that wins the awards. The Jeep keeps rolling and the cloud changes, the sunlight changes, with every kilometer and minute. This is theater. Drama without plot. Spectacle. And more important, what I retain is this memory, and the story to tell somebody else.

I can't get to my own camera fast enough, and frankly I don't want to stop. The highway comes up to an overlook above the North Saskatchewan River, and an interpretive sign tells me I'm looking at a whooping crane refuge, a flyway. The thunderhead continues to evolve, the picture it makes even better because now there's a valley and a river, a river with an island in it, green trees, fields, rolling hills, cows at rest. But the Jeep motors on. I already know this picture is a story I will try to tell, and I have no idea how to tell it.

The cloud moves east. I move west. Soon I am underneath the event and the rain settles in. Thick, gray, and heavy over everything I can see. Not a downpour, just a heavy mist. CBC radio plays something by Mendelssohn.

8:25 and on the west side of North Battleford the road again crests a hill—a valley before me and a river spread out. The Battleford bridge over the North Saskatchewan River. I know there's history here. I know there are players named Big Bear and Poundmaker, and I know this place is important in the history of western Canada. But I am very tired. My notes are few. As the sun moves lower, my desire to simply arrive grows large.

9:39 p.m. and the road approaches the Alberta border, a town called Lloydminster. There's an oil refinery at the border, the flaming top of the vent tower, lights throughout the scaffolding. Two vent towers. The Husky logo is on one of the holding tanks. It's called the Husky Lloydminster Upgrader. Across the Yellowhead, cows graze in a field.

9:56 and I am in Alberta.

10:25. Still a couple hundred kilometers east of Edmonton and I'm passing a yellow canola field on the right. The sun breaks through a band of clouds and illuminates the bottom a bright purple. The sun itself an orange red; surrounding clouds are various shades of gray to blue to nearly green. You couldn't come up with a palette to paint this. I know I'm getting tired when I start seeing shapes in the clouds—not just boats or schooners or normal things—at the moment, I see the symbol for the Klingon Federation, a uterus and fallopian tubes, and the face of Zeus.

As I roll into Edmonton at 12:05 a.m. home time, there are fireworks in the sky. Somebody's celebrating something. Red and white and green and pink balls. All sorts of fireworks and bombs.

Day Five

Day five dawns clear, bright, filled with sunshine. It's cool, but there is that feeling, that edge against the skin, that promises the day will get hot later on. Standing next to the Jeep, I pause and inhale deeply. There is a taste to the air everywhere. In Key West that taste is salt water and spice. In Montgomery, Alabama, that taste is the humidity of lush green plants. In Osage Beach, Missouri, it's the exhaust of engines. In Moorhead, Minnesota, it's the clarity of open space, unless the wind is from the north, when it carries the scent of the American Crystal sugar beet plant. Here in Edmonton, for me at least, the deep breath is flavored with anticipation and promise. I don't know what I'm smelling, what source it comes from, how many parts per billion consist of something or something else. And that unknowing feeds curiosity. Standing next to the Jeep, I know what I see and hear—the hotel and the traffic. But in my lungs now is the range of the places I can't yet see. I have a hint now, something to figure out or discover. And so I am a happy man.

Sometime today, however, I will get a call from my father. There is no doubt about his cancer. All we need to learn is the date of his operation. Every mile north on this trip is a mile farther away, a bet that medicine will move slowly. It's a bet I might lose.

When I called the hotel last night from the highway to ask for directions, the clerk couldn't tell me how to get to here. "I'm sorry," she said, over and over. "I've lived here my whole life, but I don't drive very much." She gave me some landmarks, and I finally found the place. We laughed about her directions, and then I settled in for a good night's sleep.

This morning begins with breakfast at a little family restaurant called Albert's. Denver omelet, hash browns, rye toast, and coffee. The waitress, a college-aged woman named Nedra, tall and thin, with long black hair, is a model of graciousness. Fast coffee, easy humor. She chuckles with me when I point out that one of her signs out front is misspelled—"special" is "speical." She asks where I'm heading, then wishes me luck on my trip.

At the hotel this morning, a funny conversation at the checkout desk. A woman walks up and says to the clerk, "I have a stupid question." The clerk smiles at her. The woman says, "Can you tell me where the new Krispy Kreme doughnut place is? I hear they're so popular they won't even put their number in the phone book. It's all the rage down in the States."

The desk clerk says she doesn't know, and I start to laugh. Both women look at me, wondering. So I explain that Krispy Kreme has a wonderful marketing department. I tell them the story about the store opening in Fargo. The opening was an event, a happening, a thing not to miss. They arranged for the high school orchestra to be there at six o'clock in the morning. Radio stations fell over themselves with preopening hype and then live remote broadcasts. There were crowds in the parking lot, a line of cars already queued at the drive-up window.

"Did people really camp out the night before, to be first in line?" the woman asks. I say, "Yup, they did. But you know what?" Both women lean in a bit. "They're not really all that good."

The front desk clerk goes back to her paperwork. The other woman looks at me, crestfallen. I think I've disappointed her. I think I've destroyed some kind of hope. I suddenly feel guilty of something hard. She never does find out exactly where it is.

∼

Yesterday I drove 1,062 miles from my home in Moorhead, Minnesota, to the Comfort Inn near the West Edmonton Mall in Edmonton, Alberta. And I'm tempted to drive over there this morning. It's still the world's largest shopping mall. Indoor water park, ice rink, submarines, thrill rides, and more than eight hundred stores. I do not like malls, and I do not like shopping. But this place is on a different scale. This is not shopping. This is theater. I could take a scuba lesson there. I could buy things to bring home. Souvenirs. Proof I was here. But once the Jeep is running and I'm settled into my seat, the wheels turn toward the highway.

Today I will join the Alaska Highway, the one last, great road in North America. Today I will start winding my way toward mountains, valleys, rivers and streams, and fish I can bother—stories of exploration and stories of winter.

At an Esso station, the owner has to come out from a back room because the clerks aren't sure how to ring up a manual sale for my card. He asks where I'm going, and I tell him Prudhoe Bay. "Why?" he asks. "Just to see what it's like," I say. He smiles at me. The clerks nod. I tell him I've been up the Dempster Highway in the Yukon and Northwest Territories—a couple of times, in fact—and a young female clerk perks up and says, "I know where that is! I used to live in the Faros." We talk about how pretty the land is up there. Then she has to help another customer. As the manager finishes the telephone authorization of my card, I am struck again by the idea of welcoming the traveler. The hotel desk clerks, Nedra waiting tables at Albert's, and now these gas station attendants. Every single one of them is doing the job, certainly. But there's a way to be more than efficient. Welcoming the traveler, providing not only succor but sympathy and patience and humor and help, is in fact not efficient at all. But it is deep. The conversations may be fast and slight. But the evidence of one person knowing the needs of another person and offering one's spirit is deep.

Two kilometers out of Edmonton, and raptors sit on traffic signs. Magpies flap throughout the median. An oil well churns round and round in a field on the north side of the highway. I pass a large RV with license plates from Maryland. Quickly the borders of the Yellowhead highway change from mostly fields to mostly forest. Then I exit on Route 43, north toward Whitecourt, Valleyview, and Grande Prairie. Up the road are the town of Dawson Creek and the beginning of the Alaska Highway.

It is another day in the North American prairie, although I can see the transition beginning. Still hay bales, still golden fields of canola. But just to the west there are mountains. An auto transport carries new Ford pickups, Dodge Grand Caravans, Plymouth Neons to some car dealer farther north. We're all following a member of the RCMP, driving a bit more slowly than we normally would. When he exits to the right, everybody on Route 43 goes just a little faster. I pass a mower crew working the middle of the highway. Route 43 is a four-lane divided highway. The crew works the median, doing the endless work of keeping the highways organized. And I suddenly wonder how many men and women in North America, from Mexico to Prudhoe Bay, go to work each day to make the roads, to maintain the roads, to keep the roads safe, to keep the roads pretty, to keep the roads fast. I doubt that number is on any-body's desk. I remember once trying to find out how many cars and trucks and motorcycles and whatever else were on the road at any given time in North Dakota. All I wanted was an average. On any given day, at any given time, how many engines were turning? I called the state highway office, and they couldn't begin to guess. If I gave them a specific road, a specific *stretch* of road, and a particular time on a particular day, well then they had some data. That information was useful. People had asked for it before. But no one else had ever wondered about the larger picture. No one else had any need for a larger view. My phone call was bounced from office to office. "Can you guess?" I asked half a dozen state highway officials. "No," each one of them said.

I pass more oil wells in the fields, some churning, some not. I know there are mountains to the west, though I may not see them today. I also know the natural gas that feeds the boiler that heats the water that keeps my office warm in the winter is brought up out of the earth somewhere around here. The gas that feeds the furnace in my home is Canadian gas. Between here and there, there are gas companies, pipeline com-panies, public utilities, agreements between provinces, treaties between nations. The connections are endless.

The radio brings me news of a forest fire out of control near Van-couver and describes how the smoky haze covers the area down there. Roads are closed. Breathing is difficult. There are fires in Alaska as well. Big ones. And tonight I will use my computer to check the fire maps, to see where the roads may be blocked, to get a glimpse of the danger. I will check the road condition reports and the weather reports. From the warmth of a hotel room and in the afterglow of a hot meal, I'll use computers and satellites and Doppler radar to show me a possible fu-ture. I'll see what's in front of me.

But I won't see everything. There's the present world in front of me, and there's the invisible world as well. Not ghostly or supernatural, just invisible and very real. In front of me there are names. Alaska Highway. George Dawson. Robert Service. Jack London. Yukon Territory. Yukon River. Klondike River. Northwest Territories. Alaska. Denali. Brooks Range. Prudhoe Bay. Point Barrow. Muskeg. Permafrost. Polar bear. Caribou. Beluga whale. Each name holds history and weight. Each name sparks some want in me to see, to touch, to taste and smell and hear.

North of Edmonton, and I'm moving into another history, another landscape.

~

When the road crests a small ridge near the town of Mayerthorpe, I can see off in the northwestern distance the first thing that might be honestly called a hill, a small summit, something more than just the swelling of the earth, a rise, a ridge, a bump. And I've been waiting for the mountains. I've been waiting for the way mountains can call up new emotions, new ways of seeing distance, new ways to think about size and weight and scale. The road itself continues fairly straight, with small dips, small rises, just rolling woodland and pastureland. But this morning I can see the first hints of the change. The signs for animal crossings now show the picture of a moose.

Passing the town of Blue Ridge, I see the landscape has now become all forested. I see the first highway warning sign for logging trucks: both long and wide loads, it says. An empty logging truck, looking like some type of rusted skeleton, is stopped at an Esso station as I pass.

What can I say about logging in Alberta and over in British Columbia? What can I say about logging anywhere at all? There is a lot of it. On both sides of this roadway the forests seem neatly arranged, because they are. Uniform rows of pine trees planted since the last harvest. Wood for homes and for paper, and homes for animals. There is, for example, a company called Canfor that cuts a lot of trees, and that halts operations where a caribou herd is threatened. It's not an easy issue. People need wood and paper. The ground and the animals need the trees. There are lawsuits and agreements, employment and deaths.

This is a land where superlatives are easy if not required. I pass a billboard that promises the "Coldest Beer on the Planet" at the CJ's convenience store.

When I get to Whitecourt, I see auto dealers, a Super 8, McDonald's, and Taco Time. On the north side of town the road goes down into a valley where there's a large plant—steam rising from smokestacks—and a bridge over the McLeod River. I don't see any sign to tell me what kind of plant that is, but my guess is that it is some kind of a lumber mill or maybe a paper plant, although it doesn't seem big enough for a paper plant.

I pass a sign that says "Moose Row. Save our wildlife and yourself. Drive with care." And then a thrill. The first real downgrade on this highway is very brief. It takes me across something called Chickadee Creek. A slight sweep to the left, over the creek, and then back up to the right. I find myself smiling just at the fun of it all. I'm passed by a red Chevrolet with Virginia license plates.

Nothing on either side of the road except unbroken forests. Before the town of Fox Creek, there's a 6 percent downgrade, and I let the Jeep run down it fast. Bright yellow road sign in the shape of a moose reminds me that this is Moose Row. In winter, I've been told, the plows clear the road, and the moose find it easier to walk on the road than through drifts. Fast trucks and slow moose often come close.

The tourist information center in Fox Center is in a building underneath an old oil drilling platform. Most of the trucks are tandem tankers or logging trucks. At a Fox Creek Husky Petro Canada station, the conversation is about some local event that's been rained out so often they are going to change the name. The woman behind the counter has a laugh that fills the store, and the three or four men in line laugh with her. They aren't going anywhere.

Small access roads lead away from the highway to what appear to be pipeline stations or wellheads. Hidden, mostly, by a line of trees between the sites and the highway, they would be easy to miss. It would be easy to say this is nearly wilderness. But there is industry here, and a large, complicated infrastructure just off the roadway.

A sign encourages me to report a poacher. I pass a small tank farm for Peace Pipeline, Ltd. A short while later I pass a holding area for drilling equipment. The lowlands here are wet and marshy. The pine forests straight. The pine is mixed with aspen and birch, poplar, and some other tree I can't quite make out.

At noon I pass two trucks, both pulling rvs, heading south. The first has a license plate from North Dakota. The second from Minnesota. Fifteen minutes later, I pass a car with a license plate for the Northwest Territories, a license plate in the shape of a polar bear. Outside the town of Debolt, a herd of bison graze in a field on the east side of the highway.

Shortly after one o'clock and I pass a pullout, an area for truckers to put on their tire chains. It's not much in the middle of a dry summer afternoon, just an extra wide shoulder to the roadway. Still, there is that

168

hint, that evidence of another season, another reality here. There are bright, cold days here, and days when gray clouds pour snow over the hills. The road begins to dip into a wide, broad valley. Cliffs and escarpments, rock faces, a good steep grade going downhill. My ears pop as the air pressure changes. The road sweeps left, then right, then left again through stands of birch and aspen. The Smoky River sits at the bottom of this valley. Rock shores, brown water. The blood from roadkill stains the highway past the river bridge. Then there's a chain-off area on the far side of the valley.

1:32 and I pull into the town of Grande Prairie. I don't know its population, but this is a small city. Fast-food chains. A good many hotels. Traffic lights and buildings that crowd each other. I am anxious to get through it, even though a sign tells me Grande Prairie is home of the World Chuck Wagon champion, Kelly Sutherland.

～

Coming in from the south, the first view of Dawson Creek, British Columbia, is nothing special. Buildings and homes, stores and gas stations. A line of hotels. McDonald's. When I round the bend and the town becomes visible at the bottom of a valley, I also see a small airplane, white against the blue sky, descending toward the landing strip. The road winds down through the hills, up a rise, and then down again.

You wouldn't think this was anyplace special. You wouldn't think there was a good story here. But the road leads easily through the strip of hotels and shops to a roundabout. And there at the corner is a sign. Tall, curved at the top like an arch, it marks a beginning. The world-famous Alaska Highway.

I pull into the parking lot and get out of the Jeep. The sign is behind me, and the Visitor Center just in front. There are lots of people walking about. Most of them are old enough to be retired. Some are just starting the trip. Others just ending. This is the place where the story gets framed.

I walk to the Visitor Center and linger in the gift shop for a minute. There is an information desk here, with two young women working. Men and women thumb through the racks of postcards and books and T-shirts and hats. One woman is buying sweatshirts for her whole family. Each has "Alaska Highway" in large letters across the front. Eventually everyone in the place makes their way to the desk. Those who are outbound ask the same question. "How is the road?" Those who are done wait for one of the women to reply, then offer their own confirmation or particular detail.

"How is the road?" asks one man. I saw him in the parking lot. He was posing for photographs with his family under the sign. He put his foot up on the curb the way hunters on safari used to put a foot on the head of a lion or tiger they'd killed. Triumphant. His kids stood on a large rock and raised their arms to point at the sign, as if to say, "This is where we are, and this is where we're going." His wife simply stood there and smiled. Still, I couldn't help noticing the background to their photographs. In the foreground, the adventurers. In the middle ground, the sign, the evidence of their progress. In the background, another sign. A Chevy dealer.

"There is some construction at Johnson's Landing," one woman says, "a little other construction at various places; but otherwise the road is good."

Another man, his voice thick with a southern accent, says, "It didn't take us more than thirty minutes to get through that place. Nothing to it."

"What about the fires?" asks another man. "What about the fires in Alaska? Are they still burning? Are the roads still closed?"

"The good news," the lady says, "is that the fires in Alaska have subsided. They're not out, but the roads are open there." Three or four people breathe sighs of relief.

Inside the Visitor Center, people share where they're going, how far, how many spare tires they're carrying, how much extra gasoline and water. Just giving witness, I think, to their part in the story. People who don't know each other, who ten minutes ago wouldn't have shared information with a stranger, talk about their routes, where they're staying, what they're doing, why they're on the road. This is one of the few roads left where the road itself is the destination. This is still the road people dream of while sitting at their office desks or standing knee deep in dirty laundry. This is the Alaska Highway, the road that still promises adventure and risk and beauty. A few blocks away, in the middle of town, is the official marker for Mile 0. Here at the Visitor Center there are license plates from New York, Arizona, Missouri, Nova Scotia, British Columbia.

Dawson Creek is hardly an adventurous town anymore. It's got a Wal-Mart. They're building a multiplex. It's got McDonald's. There are cappuccino shops and bakeries. But the echo is strong. This is the place where everything began.

The Alaska Highway is just one of those roads. Like Route 66, there are echoes and rumors and stories still alive in living rooms and magazines. People have heard of this road, even if those people are in Tuscaloosa or Northampton. What they've heard is that this road is wild. They've heard there's danger. Not from bandits or thieves, but from isolation, exposure, breakdown, grizzly bear and blizzard. People swear they'll never go near it, and people swear they can't wait for the chance. Everyone seems to know the road was built fast, unbelievably fast, during World War II. Everyone seems to know this road is a thrill.

In the Visitor Center I buy a book, *The Trail of '42*, and then sit on a bench outside to read. It's a warm summer afternoon. I learn that the United States bought Alaska from Russia in 1867, and people started talking about the possible trails and roads and railways north. There was even a plan to join Russia and Alaska with a railway bridge, until Russia lost the Russo-Japanese War in 1904 and Japan didn't think the bridge was a good idea. There were trails for the gold miners. But it was difficult to get supplies and people north. And national defense became a tremendous issue, for Canada as well as the United States. A string of air bases, which came to be known as the Northwest Staging Route, was established at Grande Prairie, Fort Nelson, Watson Lake, and Whitehorse. Japan didn't like this idea either, and it claimed the bases were part of an American attempt to encircle Japan. When the Japanese attacked Pearl Harbor, one of the many things that became clear was the need to supply western Canada and Alaska.

I learn that there were competing proposals for which route the road should take. The Prairie Route, proposed by the U.S. Army Corps of Engineers, became the selection. It connected the air bases and followed mostly level ground. The route was chosen on February 2, 1942. The orders to build were given on February 11. On March 2, 1942, the first troops got off the train at Dawson Creek. In June, the Japanese attacked two of the Aleutian Islands: Attu and Kiska.

The road had begun. And it was done fast. There was a northern crew heading south and a southern crew heading north. Soldiers followed old trails and sometimes climbed trees to determine a route. The bulldozers crashed through the forest. In summer there were heat and bugs and muskeg. In winter there was cold. Deep cold. Men died when their rafts overturned. Men simply froze to death. The road was just a pioneer road. Single lane and difficult. It would flood or wash out. There was a hill, a very steep grade, that the soldiers named Suicide Hill. But on October 20, 1942, the crews working south from Whitehorse met the crews working north from Dawson Creek at Contact Creek. The official time was eight months and twelve days. A ceremony was held at Soldier's Summit on November 20, 1942. Troops and supplies could now make the journey. The adequate defense of western Canada and Alaska was possible.

The pioneer road was not a good road, however. And every year some improvements were made. Grades were lessened. The road was widened. New, better paths were selected and then carefully put in. Every year, from then until now, the road has been worked on.

Looking up from the book, it seems a very long time ago. The pavement here is unbroken. There are grocery stores and sporting goods shops. There are fancy hotels and very good restaurants.

But even the story of the Alaska Highway is sitting on top of another story of this place. The town of Dawson is named after George Dawson. So is the town of Dawson Creek. So is the Dawson Hotel. So is the George Dawson this and the George Dawson that. Like Lewis and Clark, the man is everywhere. I have a book at home. *Report on an Exploration in the Yukon District, N.W.T. and Adjacent Northern Portion of British Columbia 1887, by George M. Dawson, D.S., F.G.S.* The book isn't a journal like the story of Lewis and Clark and the Corps of Discovery. There's no mention of mosquitoes, no attacks by grizzly bears, no wondering which fork of the river to take. As it says, the book is a report. Geology, topography, hydrology, anthropology. The author has been called the most outstanding scientist Canada has ever produced. He explored nearly all of western Canada, a great deal of it on foot. But he was no giant. He was no bear of a man daring the wilderness to defeat him. George Dawson had Pott's disease, a tuberculosis of the spine causing a chronic chest weakness and a humped back. As a grown man, he was the size of a ten-year-old boy. The natives called him Skookum Tumturn, which means a brave, cheery man. His first work was *Report on the Geol-*

ogy and Resources of the Region in the Vicinity of the 49th Parallel from the Lake of the Woods to the Rocky Mountains, and it announced to the world that here was genius. He found the first dinosaur fossil in Canada. His maps were extraordinary. He named peaks after his assistants as a way of thanking them, and his journals include poetry. As far as I can tell, Dawson first visited this site that would come to bear his name in 1879 when he was surveying for the railroad, trying to find a route through the Rockies. Sixty years later, when the troops arrived to begin the Alcan Railroad, the rails went no farther than Dawson. I don't have a copy of his report to the railroad. But I do know the man went much farther than here. His report on the Yukon and Northwest Territories ranges widely, in terms of miles covered and in terms of the observable world. He was a surveyor, a geologist, a botanist, an anthropologist, and a poet. More simply, he was curious. In this respect I believe he was a giant. He was ferociously curious.

～

3:38 local time and the Jeep heads west out of Dawson Creek on the Alaska Highway. Past the KFC. Past the Ford dealership. Past Boston Pizza, the Home Supply Center, and the Peace Villa motel. Past the Ramada Limited. I shouldn't make fun of it, I know. A lot of people come up here precisely for this road, and a lot of people give rise to a lot of services. But part of me wishes this was a two-rut road, or at least gravel, not a well-paved highway. I'd rather be worried about my canteen than my cappuccino. But that's the way it goes. There are as many ways to travel this road as there are people who travel it. I pass a bicyclist sitting in the grass on the shoulder eating a candy bar. His bike points west. There's an RV behind me, a motorcyclist two vehicles in front. On this road, frankly, I wouldn't be surprised to see a pogo stick.

Back at the Visitor Center, an older couple talked about coming up for the road. Now that they were retired, they were going to go fishing. They didn't know where they're going fishing, other than they were just going to go fishing, stopping at every place they could, and then, when they got to Alaska, go deep-sea fishing.

You'd hardly think this is the beginning of the big adventure. Tractors pull brush hogs mowing the sides of the highway. The view is canola and grains. Logging trucks roll by easily. This could be Iowa, except that there's no corn and a lot more trees. The first sign that something is unique about this road is the Kiskatinaw bridge. A sign points off the pavement to the original route. The bridge, curved and wooden, is the only original bridge still in use on the highway. I take the turnoff, and when the highway dips down toward the bridge, which is itself several hundred feet above the river, my ears pop from the pressure change.

Back on the main route, a sign tells me an "extreme grade" is coming up. There's a place for truckers to check their brakes. The truckers all check their brakes and traffic comes to a standstill. 7 percent, 6 percent, 5 percent, 6 percent—those are the grades a sign tells me will be coming up in the next series of valleys. The first is a 6 percent downgrade for three kilometers. The scenery from the top is like looking at the Dakota Badlands, although much larger and from much higher up. Brown hills, green grassy tops, forests of birch, aspen. There's a long line of us going downhill. Two semis each pull halves of a double-wide trailer home. Marker cars run before and after them, flashing lights for the extra wide load. We're all creeping downhill at 25 miles an hour. On the uphill side, a Brinks armored car labors by. Slowly we wind around. I can see the Peace River at the bottom of the valley. A large, what I call an upside-down bridge (the support girders are all underneath the pavement) spans the gorge. Gas pipeline towers are painted aircraft red and white.

On this roadway winding down to the bridge, I notice something on my odometer. Some time ago I learned that, on average, the center of the earth is 3,959 miles from the surface. It's a number that's stuck in my head. I don't know if that's from sea level or for some average. But back in Key West I took note of the odometer and wondered. Driving from Key West, how far until I'd reach the equivalent of the center of the earth? Outside Dawson Creek, British Columbia, traveling at twenty miles an hour on a 6 percent downgrade toward a river named Peace and a blue upside-down bridge, I pass that mark.

No molten lava here, no spinning core of solid iron. Just a river and hills, forests, and the Alaska Highway. This isn't the center of the earth. But maybe, just maybe, I think, in terms of hope and our imagination this highway is as necessary as the iron core of our planet.

The little town of Taylor rests at the base of the bridge. White towers support a natural gas pipeline. Flames top a vent shaft on the far end of the bridge. Some kind of processing plant for the natural gas. There is a strong smell of natural gas in the air. The trucks with the double-wide move much slower on the uphill side. The Jeep flies up like an airplane.

4:40 in the afternoon. The town of Fort St. John comes and goes, and then there are sailboats moored on Charlie Lake, smooth and bright in the afternoon sunshine. The Alaska Highway is just a thin ribbon of pavement through the forest. Every now and then, though, the smell of natural gas takes over the air. Access roads lead to hidden substations. Signs along the roadway are few, but there's custom sawing at one place, pilot and hotshot services at another. A sign by the roadside tells me when there's a compressor station.

Still just meandering through hills, I pass a road-killed moose. But my mind isn't really here. Soon I have to call home. Sometime today, I'm not sure when, my father was going to talk to his doctor. Sometime today, he finds out when the surgery will happen. The tests have said the cancer has not spread. But it still needs to come out. As quickly as possible. It's very possible I will turn around. It's very possible I won't finish this trip. On the phone my mother tells me I don't have to come back. She says they understand the distance, and the one chance I have. But there isn't any question. At one level, of course, this trip is a selfish lark. I'm here because no one else needs me to be anywhere else. When my father gets put on a gurney, I plan to be there.

～

5:39 in the afternoon. The radio scans the frequencies. Nothing here is strong enough to lock in. No cell phone service. Signs along the road say, "Do not enter. No parking. Poisonous H_2S gas." Other signs say "Forests forever" and declare when the forests here were logged and re-seeded. Every now and then an access road opens up, and I can peer into the forest a bit to see the metal works of the pipeline. Or a logging road heads off, gravel and dirt heading into the distance. After the poisonous H_2S gas sign, another one says, "Authorized Personnel Only."

I crest a rise where the forest clears for just a moment, and for the very first time on this entire trip I can see mountains, true mountains, to the west. They are too far away to tell if they're snowcapped or not. This time of year and this location, probably not. But there they are, nonetheless. The road dips back down into a valley and into the pine forest. I lose sight of the mountains. I realize I've been waiting for them for days. The mountains are the evidence that I'm no longer at home. Another rise, and for a brief moment I can see the Alaska Highway both in front and behind me for some distance, and I discover I'm the only one here. No other cars, no other traffic. I am surprised at my own reaction. Glee! I laugh out loud.

This is the first time for a very long while, and certainly on this trip, that I've not been within a quarter mile of another person. When I lay my head down to rest in a hotel, for all I know there's another body four feet away on the other side of the wall. Through the Everglades and the southern mountains and the prairie, there's always been another car, whether it's been the heavy traffic of I-70 across Missouri or the more lonely but still communal I-29 north through South Dakota and North Dakota. There's always been somebody. It's only 5:40 in the afternoon. I left a whole crew of people milling around in Dawson Creek. Yes, they were driving the highway. Yes, they couldn't wait to get started; but perhaps tomorrow, perhaps not in the late afternoon. So I have the road to myself for a while. I top another small rise. There's a microwave tower to the left. The "Forests Forever" sign lets me know this place was reforested in 1989. The road is paved.

~

What does it mean to explore these days? Are we old enough now, and are there enough of us now, that the only places still fresh, still unstoried, still open to wonder and magic are deep in the oceans or beyond our own moon? I am alone on the Alaska Highway, a good long distance from anywhere else. But this road has history. I am a traveler here, yes. But not an explorer. I am in the boreal forest, the taiga, that great belt of trees that circles the planet. If I put a Start sign in Alaska, I'd follow the trees through the United States, Canada, Norway and Sweden and Finland, Russia and China before I got to the Finish sign. Twelve million square kilometers. One third of the earth's total forest land. But I am a long way from the first person here. While I am looking at a forest, I am also looking at a crop. These trees are owned, and they will be cut down. Seedlings will take their place, and the circle will start again. I am also moving across land where the first people were called Athapaskan,

Sekani, Tagish, Kaska, Tutchone. Look up any of these words and you find history, art, politics, language, culture.

So if I am exploring, and I believe I am, what question, what curiosity am I chasing?

Another rise, and the mountains are straight in front of me. A sign reminds me to watch for moose the next twenty kilometers. I pass a place called the Sasquatch Crossing Lodge (where the ad promises daily Sasquatch sightings) and head downhill. Only at the bottom do I learn I've just come down Suicide Hill.

I pass another road-killed moose. A few minutes later I meet a lone bicyclist heading east, coasting downhill. Then I come to another area for truckers to check their brakes. A big drop coming up. Check your brakes; chain up here in the winter. "Very steep hill," the sign says; 9 percent grade. So down we start. I slow and upshift to third gear. "Slow," the sign says, "Very Dangerous Curve." My ears pop again. The road bends to the left. There's a cut in the guard rail where somebody's gone through, and then another one a little farther on. Then the bridge over the Sikanni Chief River.

On the far side of the bridge are a small store and campground. I buy some water and use the pay phone outside to call home. My father's surgery is scheduled for Monday.

In the store, I tell the lady I'd like to stretch my legs a little bit, and I ask about fishing in the river. She points to a gravel road just one hundred yards up the hill from the campground. She says, "You can take that road. It comes down to the back of our property. It's the old Alaska Highway." "Will it take me to Alaska?" I ask. She laughs and says, "No. Not anymore."

I take the road anyway. It's just hard-packed dirt, rutted. It takes me to where there was once a bridge. Steel pillars, stanchions, still stand in the stream. The river banks are all gravel. I hike over the gravel, unpack and assemble my fly rod, then tie on a fly called a Chernobyl ant. The new bridge, the one I crossed over, is a couple of hundred yards downstream. The water is clear and shallow and fast. There is another truck parked back here, but I don't see any people. In the *Milepost* guidebook, I learned that this water joins the Prophet River and the Muskwa River to make the Fort Nelson River. The Fort Nelson River joins the Liard, which empties into the Mackenzie, which ends at the Arctic Ocean near

Inuvik in the Northwest Territories. I learned that one of the largest ichthyosaur fossils ever found was found in the banks of the Sikanni Chief River. I learned that "ichthyosaurs looked a little bit like large, ugly dolphins."

Three or four casts and I can feel the familiar rhythm come back to my arm, the patient back cast, the gentle placement of the fly. My father's surgery is Monday, I think. At this river, I am three road-days away from Kansas City. I have four days to get there. I will not make Prudhoe Bay.

I fish for half an hour or so and nothing rises. No trout. No grayling. No pike. But each cast is a hope, a potential, a wish. A fisherman has faith in what *might* be there, a trust in the potential, an eagerness for what may be coming next. The evergreens are bright against the hills, and the water rushing over the rocks sparkles. This is a beautiful place, and I am not wasting time.

At the Buckinghorse River, I stop and try to fish again. No luck. After twenty minutes I pack up and head west again. I'm feeling anxious about time, as if I could finish this trip if I just hurried a bit.

The Alaska Highway turns left and heads straight toward the mountains. Purple wildflowers grace the shoulders and median. The road signs for animal crossings change. It's no longer a picture of a moose. Now it's caribou. 150 kilometers to go before Fort Nelson. The sun is moving behind a set of small cumulus clouds. Not even a hint of their becoming a storm, but they throw a shadow over the roadway and the valley. Endless evergreens. With the sun behind the clouds, the mountains are no longer in silhouette, and I can see the browns of the valleys and bluffs and cliffs, the greens of the trees growing up the gentler sides. Nothing here is big enough to have snow in July, though a couple of summits are windswept and bare.

Everything I see is just a surface. Every person I meet on this trip is just a surface too. Depth requires time. Depth requires education. Depth requires experience. Depth requires commitment. But this doesn't mean the surface is without merit, that it can't support its own examination. A geologist could look at the mountain faces I see now and explain what lies underneath those mountains, how they were formed, the age of the rocks, what forces are in motion. Classroom depth applied to field surface. A photographer or a painter or a poet could describe these same cliffs and hills, what they look like, the appeal that every wrinkle and valley has for the human soul.

I stop for gas at a place called Lum N' Abner's. A small gas station and café. I just want a little bit to make sure I can make it to Fort Nelson. As I get out of the Jeep, a girl, sixteen at most, and a boy about the same age leave the gas station on a four-wheel ATV and ride across the street. I don't pay much attention except to notice they are smiling brightly. They are having fun. As I pump the gas, another boy comes out of the café, points across the street and starts laughing. The kids who left have somehow managed to tip the four-wheeler over in a mud puddle, and the boy is shaking the mud off himself. The girl simply stands there, looking down at her soaked jeans and shirt. When I go inside the store to pay, they are still laughing about it. "Did they wipe out?" I ask. The cashier says, "I think they knew they were going to do that the minute they left." A man eating dinner looks up and says, "I think they're just strange on a number of levels." The woman working the till laughs and agrees. Standing there, I feel oddly included. These people know I'll be gone in five minutes, and in all likelihood they'll never see me again in their lives. So we have these five minutes. Unguarded. Not profound or devastating or approaching rapture. Just open. Familiar.

8:15 p.m. and I pass over my patch of Alaska Highway gravel. "Extremely dusty," the sign warns me. "Drive with lights on." I pass over it in a flash, and an explosion of white leaps up behind me.

I'm not sure how the distinction is made, but a sign welcomes me to the northern Rockies. "Loose gravel. Bumpy Road. Eight percent downgrade." Not bad at all, I think. The Prophet River parallels the highway now, and I pass an open-base camp for highway workers. Basically a semitrailer divided into sleeping compartments for highway workers or perhaps oil crew members. It's too far to get here from anywhere more permanent, and too far to get home again at night.

9:27 p.m. and I come around a bend. The sun is low, but still over the mountains, and the top of a smokestack appears almost like chrome in the sunlight. It's not chrome, of course. It's concrete. There's some kind of a white wrapping at the top. The stack rises from the Fort Nelson generating station. There's a vent pipe with fire on top. Duke Energy, the sign says. Gas processing plant. Gas transmission. I smile at first impressions. For one brief moment, that chrome glow in the sky appeared as alien as a spaceship.

As I pull into Fort Nelson, the sun is low enough that the clouds above me are lit from underneath, amber and gold upside-down peaks, dark indigo blue in the cloud valleys where the sun has yet to reach.

Day Six

8:53 in the morning and I'm heading north out of Fort Nelson. This will be my last day on the road north. Tomorrow I begin the race back to Kansas City for my father's surgery. I have half a day to head north, then half a day to get back here.

I need a fishing license, so I stop at a place called CMP Sports and the clerk tells me that Tetsa River is a good place to try, as well as the Toad River and a few others. My goal today is to get into the mountains, to feel that kind of air on my face and neck. I hope to make it to the Morley River bridge today, where in the past the fish have been generous and willing. It's a favorite spot of mine, one of those places the imagination holds and can call up easily. Dense evergreen forest comes down the hills to the water's edge. The bridge is only an eyeblink on the highway, but just upstream is a wide pool with a sandy bank to wade in. Casting from the pool back under the bridge, where all the bugs fall in the water, has been one of those stories we live and then bother other people to hear a thousand miles away. Monster fish rise from the streambed to sip at a fly, and then the dance of bringing one in. Every fish I have caught there I have let go. Still, I may not make the Morley River today. The bridge is six or seven hours in front of me, and then it's six or seven hours back.

North out of Fort Nelson the Alaska Highway takes a turn to the left, and suddenly the real mountains are in front of me. Occasional signs for the old Alaska Highway point off into the bush either to the right or to the left. But those are for days when I have time. I pass a sign that says "Forestry renewal: an enhanced forestry project." Forests of birch, aspen, and pine on both sides of the highway.

9:37 and the road climbs steadily into the foothills. The valleys are now behind me. Summit Lake is only fifty-four kilometers in front of me. Passing a place called Steamboat, a valley opens up to my left, a deep, broad valley, and I'm shocked at how high up I already am. Suddenly the twists are tighter in the road, and the posted speed limit for curves goes way down. Without much warning, I am suddenly in the mountains. I imagine a contour line on some map that shows I'm following a well-defined route, a gentle gain in elevation, the easiest way for truck and transport. I've been driving through a small pass. But through a trick of perspective, the road turns and it appears as if there's a whole mountain range suddenly behind me. I know they are just to the south, the mountains I was paralleling before. But to see them in the rearview mirror makes me wonder what I missed. After Steamboat, a little more rise and a pass, then the Alaska Highway begins to descend, following that contour line down into the next valley. The first range of the foothills has been crossed. A long way from home, and a very long way from Key West, I am in the Canadian Rockies at last. I am in the *northern* Canadian Rockies.

9:50 in the morning and I pull off for the Tetsa River Provincial Park, the first place the guy back at the CMP Sports told me to go fishing. A gravel road leads two and a half kilometers off the highway down to the park and is bordered by arctic cotton and fireweed. There's a sign at the entrance to the park that says "A fed bear is a dead bear. Bears that associate food with people are dangerous and must be destroyed. Do not feed the bears." At the Tetsa River Provincial Park, I fish for half an hour or so and nothing really happens. But it's a very pretty river with stony banks.

A young couple, middle to late twenties, I think, comes down to the river a hundred yards or so from where I am. They sit for a while, watching the stream, and then leave. I cast, change flies and cast again. Nothing rises. Nothing wants to strike underwater. A lull in the day. I'm going to head up north a little more. Stone Mountain is calling me. I make a mental note to try the Tetsa one more time on my way back down today.

Eleven o'clock in the morning and the road winds through the mountains. I come around a bend, and suddenly the bare top of Stone Mountain is visible in front of me. I cross the Tetsa River several times—bridge number one, bridge number two—and see the braided links of it at the side of the road. In my mind there is a small fantasy of spending real time here. Months or years. Time to learn which holes hold the real fish.

Time to see this river swell with runoff and then freeze with autumn.

Stone Mountain Provincial Park, the sign says. "Caution," the next sign says, "Caribou on Highway." Summit Lake is deep blue green against the morning sky and evergreen hills. I watch a ripple in the water for a few minutes, then realize it's a moose swimming across the lake. It's an impressive sight. I pull into the campground and take far too many pictures. I already know not one of them will hold the taste of the air, the temperature of the sky, the way my mind is counting hours spent against hours available and wishing there were more of it all. A strong wind blows from the northwest this morning. The lake is filled with tiny whitecaps. Chilly.

On the northwest side of the lake, a raven feeds on a road-killed moose. A short while after Summit Lake, it's an 8 percent downgrade through rocky cliff faces and stands of pine. A man I think is in his fifties struggles up the grade on a recumbent bicycle.

11:24 in the morning and my heart is sinking. In front of me, the clouds are coalescing. I can see rain falling. Behind me, bright blue skies and cotton-ball clouds. It's possible my one day in the mountains will turn gray and drizzly. I don't mind, though. Bad weather is good drama. I tend to like whatever comes along. When the rain does come it brings a good strong wind pushing hard through the valley. Treetops and brush bend over. But I can already see blue sky behind it. This storm will pass.

11:47 in the morning. The Toad River Lodge, a place famous because of its hat collection—more than 7,000 donated caps from celebrities and nobodies hanging from the ceiling—passes by me on the left. More than 7,000 people have been here before me. There are caps in the basement, uncounted, waiting for some day when an older one falls or is no longer interesting. Who knows how many people have come through bare-headed or felt attached enough to their cap that they refused to hand them over as an offering? I've stood under that collection. I have wished my own cap were there as a sign. A sign to someone else—someone I don't know, someone I can't even imagine properly—that I was here. I've thought there would be comfort, when the mundane and the ordinary and the perfunctory parts of my life become nearly overwhelming, in knowing that a cap of mine was hanging from the ceiling of a small café in the northern Rockies. I've thought there would be comfort in the evidence that I had done something, been someplace, large. But I've also thought there's a bit of trophyism here. Another cap in the ceiling no better than another pushpin in the map.

Another storm comes in. The road is supposed to be very dusty here, but the rain keeps the dust down. A few minutes later, the Muncho Lake Provincial Park arrives. I come around a corner and there are two caribou in the middle of the road. Both of them are skittish and jump when I slow. The rain quickly passes.

One o'clock in the afternoon and I'm fishing downstream from a bridge over the Toad River when a storm comes through. This one is a nice little storm. I could hear the wind in the valley as it built its way toward me. I see the trees at the far upstream corner of a turn in the river bend and shake in the gusts. I see the water at that bend riffle and turn gray. When the rain gets to me, I stand under the bridge and continue to cast, hopeful. But the wind keeps coming, making any cast with my fly rod a foiled attempt. I pack up the rod and sit on a rock and just watch the storm.

After lunch I realize I'm only thirty miles from the Liard River Hot Springs. I also realize my mind is no farther north. I'm no longer imagining the border with Alaska. I'm no longer imagining my friend Joe and his Widgeon, a wonderful amphibious airplane named for a duck. In my mind, I'm not dreaming of the Dalton Highway, or the Brooks Range, or the end of the road. In my mind, all I see is Kansas City and the road from here to there.

Thirty miles to the Liard River Hot Springs, I think. I'm going to dip my feet in the water there and then turn around. There are scattered thunder cells moving through the mountains.

3:15 p.m. and I cross the suspension bridge over the Liard River. Two kilometers in front me are the hot springs. I pull off the highway and into the parking area. People meander about in bathing suits, shirts open. Signs warn about grizzly attacks. A young woman, pregnant, dabbles her feet in the water. She tells me she lives just a little way up the road. Her parents are swimming in the lower thermal pool. It's their first time visiting, she says. We talked about the upper pool, talk about the bear story of several years ago, the bear that jumped in and mauled a tourist before being shot by another tourist who was then cited for having a firearm in a provincial park. When I heard the story on television, the narrator said the bear had zero percent body fat. I talk with another man who, as he gets out of the pool, mutters, "Uff da." I look at him, astounded: "Norwegian?" "No, German. I'm from Minnesota, and that's what everyone says there." We make that connection. I tell him I'm from Moorhead, and he tells me he's from Brainerd. He's coming back down the Alaska Highway. He's been up to the Kenai Peninsula fishing for halibut and salmon. It's taken him two days to get here from there. He says that if he didn't get a fish on every cast, he was doing something wrong. He says, "Whoever said hauling those fish up is like hauling up a barn door was right." He smiles as he tells me this, enjoying the fact that he could tell the story.

Men and women of all ages, in bathing suits and robes of all ages, walk up and down the boardwalk of the hot springs area. They get in the water. One woman explains, "Normally, I get in slow because the water is cold. Today I'm getting in slow . . . ." Then her friend finished, "Because it's hot!" The sky to the north is now clear blue.

I began this trip in Key West, knee deep in the Atlantic Ocean. I had hoped to end it knee deep in the Arctic Ocean. But knee deep in the hot springs of the Liard River thermal area will do nicely. I could say I'm disappointed, but that wouldn't really be true. I am sad that I will not have a chance to see Alaska, drive the Dalton, see my friends Joe and Peggy and my friend Bill who is visiting them. I am sad that I will not see the mountains I know only by name. Denali. Brooks Range. But there is tremendous grace in what may be coming. For me, those things remain in the future, a potential. I expect I will get there someday. The things we expect continue to lure us, continue to motivate us, continue to make us work hard to get there. I know more deeply the connections I have to family, the connections I have to other people. As the car points south, I know I am only a few days away from the few hours when a mortal will fit a knife in his hand and open up another mortal, to heal instead of harm, and then close him back up again. With any luck, all will be well. I do not know the details of my father's cancer. I'm sure I will find that out as quickly as he does. I do know that when he goes into surgery I will be in that room to say good-bye, and in that room to say good morning when he wakes up again.

What I do not know this afternoon, as the Jeep begins to roll south and east, is that my father will be fine. I will be there for the operation, and for several days afterward. And we will learn that the cancer hasn't spread. We will learn that the doctors got it all, that there's no need for radiation or chemotherapy. He is, in effect, cured. All better.

All I know this afternoon is that I've stopped at a road construction site, as have many others, waiting for a pilot car to lead us through the gravel and dirt. In this line of cars there are license plates from Nevada, California, Utah, British Columbia, Manitoba, Wisconsin. The pilot car arrives, and we all follow slowly.

Just on the south side of the Rocky Mountain Lodge, I stop for gas. And when I get going again, I see a semi-truck pulled into a pullout. Nothing special, I think. Then the truck driver rises from the lake and shakes water off himself like an animal. He is as naked as the day he was born.